Campaign

OSPREY
PUBLISHING

Guam 1941 & 1944

Loss and reconquest

Campaign • 139

OSPREY
PUBLISHING

Guam 1941 & 1944

Loss and reconquest

Gordon L Rottman • Illustrated by Howard Gerrard

Series editor Lee Johnson • Consultant editor David G Chandler

First published in Great Britain in 2004 by Osprey Publishing, Elms Court,
Chapel Way, Botley, Oxford OX2 9LP, United Kingdom.
Email: info@ospreypublishing.com

© 2004 Osprey Publishing Ltd.

A CIP catalogue record for this book is available from the British Library

ISBN 1 84176 811 1

Editor: Lee Johnson
Design: The Black Spot
Index by Alison Worthington
Maps by The Map Studio
3D bird's-eye views by John Plumer
Battlescene artwork by Howard Gerrard
Originated by The Electronic Page Company, Cwmbran, UK
Printed in China through World Print Ltd.

04 05 06 07 08   10 9 8 7 6 5 4 3 2 1

For a catalog of all books published by Osprey Military
and Aviation please contact:

Osprey Direct USA, c/o MBI Publishing, P.O. Box 1,
729 Prospect Ave, Osceola, WI 54020, USA
E-mail: info@ospreydirectusa.com

Osprey Direct UK, P.O. Box 140, Wellingborough,
Northants, NN8 2FA, UK
E-mail: info@ospreydirect.co.uk

www.ospreypublishing.com

Artist's note

Readers may care to note that the original paintings from which the
color plates in this book were prepared are available for private sale.
All reproduction copyright whatsoever is retained by the Publishers.
All enquiries should be addressed to:

Howard Gerrard
11 Oaks Road,
Tenterden,
Kent
TN30 6RD
UK

The Publishers regret that they can enter into no correspondence
upon this matter.

KEY TO MILITARY SYMBOLS

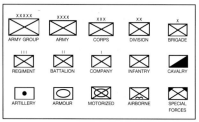

Abbreviations

AAA	anti-aircraft artillery
Adm	Admiral
amtrac	amphibian tractor (see also LVT)
AT	anti-tank
BAR	Browning automatic rifle
CINCPOA	Commander-in-Chief, Pacific Ocean Area
CO	Commanding Officer
CP	Command Post
CT	Combat Team (USMC)
DUKW	2$\frac{1}{2}$-ton amphibious truck ("Duck")
FBL	Force Beachhead Line
FMFPac	Fleet Marine Force, Pacific
HQ	Headquarters
IIIAC	III Amphibious Corps
IIB	Independent Infantry Battalion (IJA)
IMB	Independent Mixed Brigade (IJA)
IMR	Independent Mixed Regiment (IJA)
IGHQ	Imperial General Headquarters
IJA	Imperial Japanese Army
IJN	Imperial Japanese Navy
IMAC	I Marine Amphibious Corps (became IIIAC)
InfDiv	Infantry Division (US Army)
LCI	Landing Craft, Infantry
LCM	Landing Craft, Mechanized
LCT	Landing Craft, Tank
LCVPs	Landing Craft, Vehicle and Personnel
LFBL	Landing Force Beachhead Line
LSD	Landing Ship, Dock
LST	Landing Ship, Tank
LVT	Landing Vehicle, Tracked ("amtrac")
LVT(A)	Landing Vehicle, Tracked (Armored)
MarBde	Marine Brigade
MarDiv	Marine Division
MP	Military Police
NC	Naval Construction (battalion) ("Seabees")
NCO	non-commissioned officer
NTLF	Northern Troops and Landing Force
O-1	Objective 1 Line (first day's objective)
Prov	Provisional (temporary unit)
RCT	Regimental Combat Team (4th Marine and 27th InfDiv)
SNLF	Special Naval Landing Force (Japanese)
STLF	Southern Troops and Landing Force
TF	Task Force
TG	Task Group
UDT	Underwater Demolition Team
US	United States
USMC	United States Marine Corps
VAC	V Amphibious Corps
(-)	reduced (elements detached from parent unit)
(+)	reinforced (additional elements attached)

COMPARATIVE RANKS

US Marine and Army Officers	Japanese Army Officers
2ndLt: 2nd Lieutenant	SubLt: Sub-Lieutenant
1stLt: 1st Lieutenant	Lt: Lieutenant
Capt: Captain	Capt: Captain
Maj: Major	Maj: Major
LtCol: Lieutenant Colonel	LtCol: Lieutenant Colonel
Col: Colonel	Col: Colonel
BGen: Brigadier General ("one-star")	MajGen: Major General
MajGen: Major General ("two-star")	LtGen: Lieutenant General
LtGen: Lieutenant General ("three-star")	—
Gen: General ("four-star")	Gen: General

Battalions organic to US Marine and Army regiments are designated with the
battalion and regimental number, e.g. 1/9 is 1st Bn., 9th Marines and 2/306 is
2nd Bn., 306th Infantry Regiment. Companies and batteries are designated in a
similar manner, e.g. A/1/9 – Company A, 1st Battalion, 9th Marines. Japanese
battalions are similarly designated; e.g., II/18 is II Bn., 18th Regiment.

The Japanese place the surname first and the personal name second.
Contemporary and post-war writings usually reverse the two. This book follows
the Japanese practice.

CONTENTS

STRATEGIC SITUATION PACIFIC THEATER, DECEMBER 1943

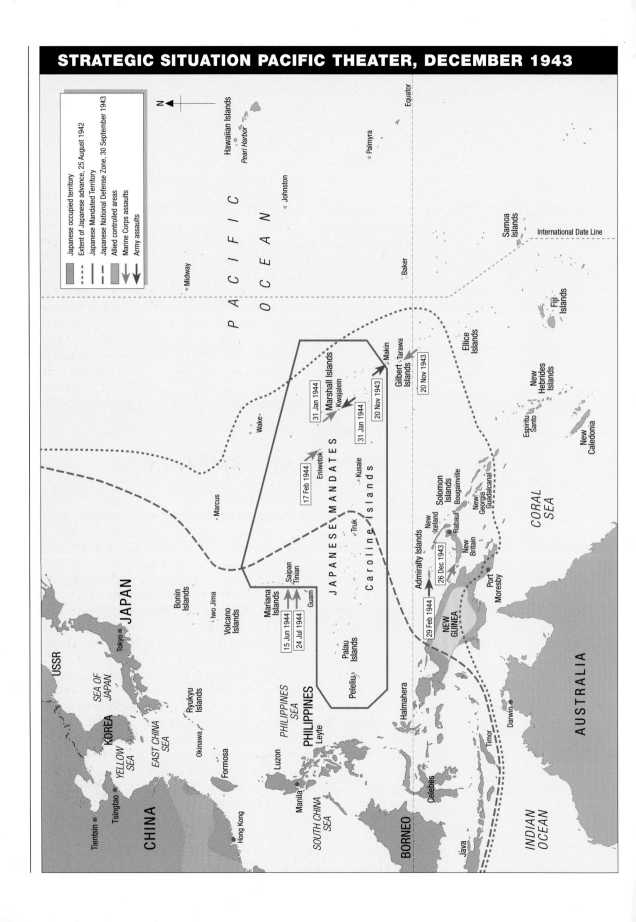

INTRODUCTION

This book studies two battles. The seizure of Guam in December 1941 was one of the Imperial Japanese armed forces' first victories in the Pacific War, known to the Japanese as the Great East Asian War. The July 1944 battle followed on the heels of the American assault on Saipan and the battle of the Philippine Sea, which advanced the US forces into the heart of Japan's pre-war territories.

In 1941 Guam was a rather exposed American possession situated at the south end of the Marianas with Saipan, a significant Japanese naval and air base, only 100 miles (161km) to the northwest. Only 400 Marine and Navy personnel and just over 300 Guamanian militia and police defended the island. Their largest weapons were a few .30cal machine guns; there were no fortifications or aircraft, and only one minesweeper. No reinforcements were planned or expected. After a token resistance the defenders went into captivity and Guam endured two and half years of repressive occupation.

ORIGINS OF THE CAMPAIGN

A series of high-level conferences, primarily between the US president, the British prime minister, and the chiefs of staff of the combined armed forces (but occasionally including other heads of state), was the mechanism for long-range planning for the Pacific War. However, the Marianas were not included among the objectives agreed at either the Casablanca Conference in January 1943 or the "Trident" Conference in May of the same year. The Navy had argued strongly at both conferences in favor of using its expanding fleets to seize the Marianas, as a springboard for the liberation of the Philippines and the invasion of Japan. General Douglas MacArthur was committed to liberating the Philippines via a drive through the Southwest Pacific, and opposed a major thrust through the Central Pacific fearing it would divert resources; thus the Navy were ignored. Ironically, the greatest champion of the Central Pacific route was one of the Navy's most vehement opponents. With the new B-29 Superfortress now available, the Air Force needed bases from which to operate these monsters. The only bases currently within range of Japan were in China, forcing the Superfortresses to operate at the limits of their capabilities. In addition, supplying the aircraft in China with fuel, spares and munitions was a logistics nightmare, and the Air Force pointed out that airbases in the Marianas would reduce the roundtrip to targets in Japan by 1,200 miles, and could be supplied direct from the United States. At the Cairo Conference ("Sextant") in December 1943, the Navy and Air Force joined forces and successfully argued that twin attacks through the Central Pacific and the Philippines was the most effective method to defeat Japan: "to

Marines outside the Marines Barracks, Sumay, Guam in 1899 soon after the United States received it as a possession. The United States paid Spain 20 million dollars for the Philippines, Puerto Rico, and Guam after winning the 1898 Spanish-American War.

obtain objectives from which we can conduct intensive air bombardment and establish a sea and air blockade against Japan, and from which to invade Japan proper if this should prove necessary." On 27 December 1943, the Central Pacific Operation Plan "Granite II" was completed with a provisional date of 15 November 1944 for the seizure of Saipan, Tinian, and Guam.

With the campaign underway the "Granite" plan almost inevitably evolved. It began precisely on schedule on 31 January 1944 with the assault on Kwajalein Atoll in the Marshalls. The speed with which this operation was completed allowed Eniwetok to be seized two months early, in February rather than May. Douglas MacArthur had not given up, however, and once again sought approval for his plan. His powers of persuasion must have been formidable as he even convinced some on Admiral Chester Nimitz's Pacific Fleet staff that an assault via New Guinea and the Philippines was preferable to a drive through the Central Pacific. However, when Admiral Earnest King, Chief of Naval Operations, was presented with the plan he rebuked Nimitz for his apparent lack of resolve. The Marianas assault was moved forward two weeks and in mid-February the "Gibraltar of the Pacific", the Japanese naval base at Truk in the central Marshalls, was neutralized in a series of attacks from the sea and air. The route to the Marianas was suddenly open and MacArthur was also able to step up his operations, seizing the Admiralty Islands at the end of February 1944. At the planning conference in Washington in February and March, the schedule for the remainder of the Pacific War was established. Numerous objectives were abandoned and many others altered with the Joint Chiefs of Staff agreeing six phases for future operations. Number 4 was, "Establishment of control of the Marianas–Carolines–Palau area by Nimitz's forces by neutralizing Truk; by occupying the southern Marianas, target date 15 June 1944; and by occupying the Palaus, target date 15 September 1944."

It would have been just as easy to secure only Guam. Politically this would have removed the stain of the US defeat in 1941, and militarily would have permitted the construction of the airfields from which to bomb Japan. Although Saipan and Tinian could have been neutralized with naval and air power, it was decided that the considerable enemy forces on the islands should be destroyed. In addition, airbases on the more favorable Tinian would be 100 miles closer to Japan.

Virtually the entire resources of Admiral Raymond A. Spruance's Fifth Fleet, elements of the Pacific Fleet Service Forces, Pacific Fleet Submarines, and South Pacific Force Land Based Air Forces; two Marine amphibious corps, three Marine divisions, two Army divisions, and a Marine brigade would be committed to Operation "Forager", the conquest of the Marianas.

Good quality intelligence was needed to support operational planning, and while Guam had been under US control for 43 years, the available information was sometimes poor and incomplete. Various pre-war studies had been accomplished to support the development of defenses on Guam and these provided some information. Maps of the island were often inaccurate in depicting roads and terrain contours, although harbor and offshore charts proved accurate enough. Another source of information were Navy and Marine personnel who had served on the island before the war. Guamanians serving in the Navy were also a valuable source. A further source, and one seldom available to planners, also proved valuable to some of the landing unit commanders. From 1936 one of the training exercises conducted by Marine Corps Schools for field grade officers was the "Guam Problem." This was a planning exercise in which officers studied the defense and capture of Guam from a hypothetical enemy. Many of the Marine commanders who would assault the island had participated in this classroom exercise and found they had a clearer picture of the terrain and natural obstacles.

The first aerial photos of Guam were taken on 25 April 1944, but clouds prevented full coverage. Additional missions in May and June provided good coverage of the landing beaches and most of the island, but it was not until after the invasion force was embarked that complete mosaic photos of the island were available. Regardless, terrain models were constructed based on these photos, but there were errors. Ground commanders often found that the terrain was rougher than expected and this could not be determined from aerial photos because of overhead vegetation. The Japanese had used the prewar American

Government House on Agaña's Plaza de Espana (Square of Spain) in 1941. This was Guam's administrative center under both the Americans and Japanese.

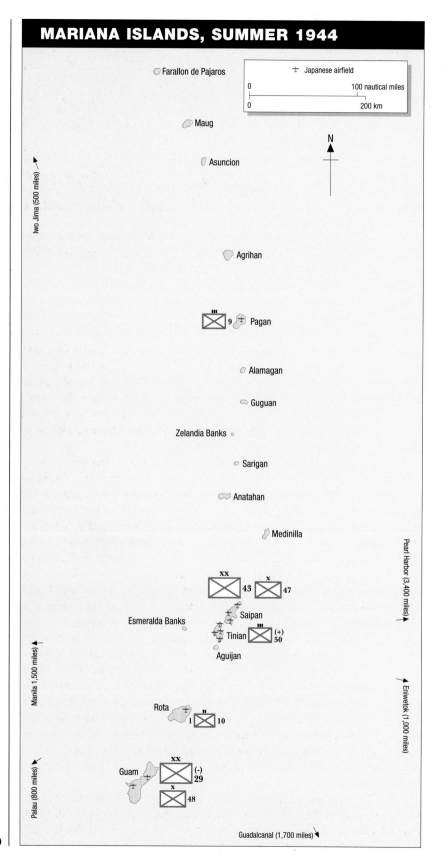

Farallon de Pajaros

✠ Japanese airfield

0   100 nautical miles

0   200 km

Maug

N

Asuncion

Iwo Jima (500 miles)

Agrihan

9 ✠ Pagan

Alamagan

Guguan

Zelandia Banks

Sarigan

Anatahan

Medinilla

Pearl Harbor (3,400 miles)

XX
43

X
47

Saipan

Esmeralda Banks

Tinian

III
(+)
50

Manila (1,500 miles)

Aguijan

Eniwetok (1,000 miles)

Rota

II
1   10

Palau (800 miles)

Guam

XX
(-)
29

X
48

Guadalcanal (1,700 miles)

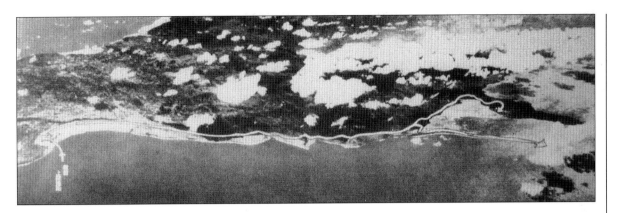

Although a little feint, the route taken by the 370-man 5th Company, *Maizuri* 2nd Special Naval Landing Force on 10 December 1941 is traced in white. It runs from the landing site at Dungcas Beach on Agaña Bay (the island's narrow isthmus can be seen in this area), follows the coast to Agaña, then to Piti Navy Yard, and then splits into two elements with one to sweep Cabras Island and Apra Harbor's breakwater and another to move onto Orote Peninsula and secure the Marine Barracks and Sumay.

survey and had produced a more accurate map. Marines and soldiers treasured captured Japanese maps. While there were inaccuracies, the available materials were sufficient for planning.

MARIANA ISLANDS

The US codename for the Mariana Islands was "Gateway", to the Japanese they were known as Mariana Shoto. The 425-mile-long (684km) chain is some 300 miles (483km) due north of the West Caroline Islands. Pearl Harbor is 3,400 miles (5,472km) to the east, Tokyo 1,260 miles (2,028km) to the north-northwest, and Manila 1,500 miles (2,414km) to the west. Some 500 miles (805km) to the northwest is Iwo Jima, the next stepping-stone to Tokyo.

The Marianas' 15 islands run north to south in a shallow curving chain, its concave side to the west, facing the Philippine Sea. Those in the north are essentially volcanic peaks while the southern islands are larger, hilly volcanic landmasses. The total land area, exclusive of Guam, is 177 square miles; Guam adds another 225 square miles. The predominating vegetation is scrub and ironwood trees, palm, and brush. Open grass-covered areas are common. Mangrove swamps are found in some coastal areas. With the exception of Guam, the islands lack streams. Wells and rain catchments provided water. Most beaches are small with the coastlines edged with coral limestone cliffs. The shorelines are closely edged by coral reefs presenting an obstacle to landings.

The northeast trade winds from December to May provide a dry season. From June to November the southwest monsoon brings between five and 15 inches of rainfall a month. Temperatures at the time of the battle ranged from 70 degrees Fahrenheit at night to the high 80s in the day with high humidity. Winds were moderate, mostly from the south, with occasional rain. Cloud cover is experienced some 60 percent of the year. This did not hamper air operations other than to cause delays in obtaining sufficient aerial photography and restricted aerial observation aircraft at times. The islands are free of most of the diseases plaguing much of the tropics.

The Portuguese explorer Ferdinard Magellan discovered the Marianas in 1521 during his first circumnavigation of the earth. Initially named *Islas de los Velas Latinas* (Islands of the Lateen Sails) after the rigging style of the native boats, they were also known as *Islas de los*

A stylized Japanese view of the occupation of Guam by the 144th Infantry Regiment, South Sea Detachment. Part of the IJN's Guam Occupation Force can be seen offshore; it consisted of four heavy cruisers, four destroyers, two gunboats, six submarine chasers, four minesweepers, and two tenders. (original painting by Ezaki Kohei)

Ladrones (Islands of the Thieves), a name commonly used into the 20th century. Spain formally claimed the islands in 1565, naming them *Las Marianas* after Queen Maria Anna in 1668. Some 75,000 Chamorros of Mayo-Polynesian descent, occupied the islands as early as 2,000BC. Modern Chamorros possess a great deal of Spanish and Filipino blood. The Chamorros rebelled against the Spanish on several occasions with the last revolt being in 1695 against the imposition of Christianity. Spain brutally put down the revolt almost wiping out the Chamorros. Little was done to develop the islands and Spain's hold on them was weak. After the beginning of the Spanish-American War, the cruiser USS *Charleston* landed a Marine detachment on Guam on 21 June 1898 and accepted the governor's surrender. The island was soon a US possession. In 1899 the remainder of the Marianas, Marshalls, and Carolines were purchased from Spain by Germany. The Japanese seized the islands in October 1914, after the beginning of World War I.

In December 1920 Japan was granted a mandate by the League of Nations to govern the former German possessions, effective 1 April 1922. In December 1914 the Japanese established the "South Seas Defense Force" to garrison what became known simply as the Japanese Mandate. The civilian-run South Seas Bureau *(Nan'yo-Cho)* was organized in 1920 and placed directly under the Ministry of Overseas Affairs. The Mandate was divided into six administrative districts: Palaus, Marianas, Marshalls; and West, Central, and East Carolines. The *Bureau* was headquartered on Koror Island in the Palaus, West Carolines. The administrative center for the Marianas District was at Garapan on Saipan. Virtually all commercial activity was under the control of the South Sea Development Company and the Nankai Trading Company.

Japan began to colonize the islands and by the late 1930s Japanese settlers outnumbered the natives. Economic exploitation was extensive including fishing, agriculture (mainly sugarcane, maize, coffee, vegetables and tropical fruits), phosphate and bauxite mining, and wood products. Japan declared the Mandate closed to Westerners in 1935 after serving its mandatory two-year notice to the League of Nations, from which it withdrew. It was not long before the popular press called the Mandate

"Japan's islands of mystery." Japan is often accused of "illegally" fortifying the Mandates, but she was under no obligation not to. The 1922 Five Power Naval Treaty was merely an agreement between Japan and the US to maintain the status quo of fortifications and navy bases in certain possessions. The Mandate was not included in the agreement.

Japan's 4th Fleet was activated on 15 November 1939 and was tasked with using amphibious and light forces to defend the Mandate. An independent defense system was established for each of the three main island groups, centered on Jaluit, Truk, and Saipan. The strategy for defending the Mandate was for 4th Fleet air and naval forces to launch raids and small-scale operations beyond the range of Allied bases and reconnaissance aircraft in order buy time for the Combined Fleet to sortie. It would then defeat the approaching US fleet in a decisive engagement.

Guam

Guam's history in the 20th century diverged from the rest of the Marianas. On 21 June 1898, during the Spanish-American War, the cruiser USS *Charleston* arrived at Guam and fired on the Spanish fort. The Spanish governor thanked the US captain for firing a salute and apologized that he was unable to return the honor as there was no powder for his guns. He was unaware that America and Spain were at war. A Marine detachment landed and the Navy was given responsibility for the island's government. A Navy captain served as the governor and commandant of the naval base, but a degree of civilian control was permitted. Guam was first a naval station, essentially encompassing the entire island and its three mile territorial limits. A navy yard was established at Piti, the port of entry, in 1899 and a Marine Barracks at Sumay in 1901. The Navy proposed defenses on Guam and in 1905 established a coaling station. In 1908 it was decided to develop Pearl Harbor but six 6in. guns were emplaced on Guam in 1909. Other proposals for Guam's defense were made before and after World War I to protect the route to the Philippines, but little was done. In 1921 a Marine seaplane unit was stationed there, the first Marine aviation unit to serve in the Pacific.

Under the terms of the 1922 Washington Navy Conference, both the US and Japan agreed not to fortify their western Pacific possessions, which had an impact on Guam's future military development. In subsequent years little was done to develop the naval station and even those guns that had been emplaced were removed by 1930. The island had no airfields and the Marine seaplane unit was withdrawn in 1931. After Japan withdrew from the League of Nations, the Navy again sought approval to fortify the island, but was told in 1938 that it would be inappropriate to make further requests of Congress. The 1939 Hepburn Board urged that Guam be developed as an advanced fleet base and the 1940 Greensdale Board recommended more modest base development. In 1941 Guam was given a Category "F" defense rating meaning that no new defenses would be established and that the naval forces would only destroy facilities and materials to prevent them from falling into enemy hands before withdrawing. Congress feared any effort to develop defenses on Guam would intimidate and provoke Japan. Some limited base improvement was approved and contract work began in May 1941.

Prior to World War II the US Government officially designated the island simply "Guam" deleting the appendages "Island" and "Mariana Islands," the latter to sever any identity with the Japanese Mandate. Located at the southern end of the Marianas, Guam's nearest neighbor is Rota Island 47 miles (76km) to the northeast and Saipan is 100 miles (161km) in the same direction.

Covering 225 square miles, Guam is the largest of the Marianas. It is 32 miles (52km) long from north to south and 10 miles (16km) wide across at its widest points. Its narrow central isthmus is four miles (6.4km) across. The north and south of the island, separated by this lowland isthmus, are very different.

A hill chain dominates the south end, running north along the west coast to Agaña, the island's main town. The hills are rugged and pitted by caves and ravines. Mount Lamlam near the lower west coast is 1,334ft (407m) high, the highest peak. Notable peaks north of Mt. Lamlam are Mounts Alifan (869ft/265m), Tenjo (1,022ft/312m), Chachao (1,046ft/319m), and Alutom (1,082ft/330m). Guam's south is covered with scrub forest and sword, cogon and bunch grass, although Mounts Lamlam, Taene, and Alifan are forested with hardwood stands. The southern valleys and coastal areas are fertile and under cultivation with rice and vegetables. The soil on the island's southern half is red volcanic clay, which turns into a thick mud after heavy rains. Numerous rivers and streams flow out of the hills to the sea with the largest, Talofofo, Ylig and Pago, flowing to the east coast. On the lower west coast, from Agaña south, are over 20 smaller rivers at between 1,000 and 3,000-yard (914–2,743m) intervals. A large swamp is located inland from the southeast coast and another swampy area is found on the west side of the isthmus along the Agaña River to the east of Agaña Town. Much of the isthmus is covered with coconut palms.

A 400–500ft (122–152m) high limestone plateau covers the island's north. Its rolling terrain is broken by Mounts Barrigada (674ft/205m) and Santa Rosa (870ft/265m)) on the central upper east coast and Machanao (610ft/186m) at the north end's Ritidian Point. The north consists of extremely dense tropical forest and undergrowth making off-trail movement difficult.

From Tumon Bay (on the west coast just north of the isthmus) around the north end and down the east coast to Pago Bay, the northern coral reef-fringed coastline is edged with 100–600ft (31–183m) limestone cliffs. As with the hinterland, the southern coast is very different from the northern. The southern east coast is also fringed with a narrow coral reef, but the cliffs are lower and there are breaks in them. Heavy surf beats the south and southeast coasts, and the former has rugged offshore reefs reaching out over 2 miles (3.2km). Low, barren and surrounded by a reef, Cocos Island lies about 2,000 yards (1,829m) off the southwest end of Guam and is some 2,500 yards (2,286m) long. The southwest coast is faced with low cliffs rising directly into the hills, as such the road system in this area is particularly poor.

The only part of the island that possessed suitable landing beaches, of sufficient width and depth with narrow reefs, was a 15-mile (24km) stretch of the central portion of the lower west coast. The reefs are between 25 and 700 yards (23–640m) wide, but there are numerous gaps. Jutting out from the center of this coast is the 4-mile (6.4km) long Orote Peninsula. Apra

MajGen Horii Tomitaro, commanding the 55th Infantry Group and the South Seas Detachment, was responsible for seizing Guam.

Harbor, or San Luis d'Apra, lies on the peninsula's north side and Agat Bay on its south. Near its base in an area of rice paddies, the peninsula is about $^1/_2$-mile (805m) wide; it widens to between $^3/_4$ and 1 mile and then tapers to a point. It is fronted with 100–200ft (31–61m) high cliffs on both sides. Most of the peninsula was covered with scattered palms and scrub brush, except around the planned Orote Airfield at the western end. A mangrove swamp is situated on the peninsula's north shoulder. Off the peninsula's west end is Orote Island and off its south-central coast is Neye Island, small rocky islets less than 100 yards (91m) offshore.

Apra Harbor on the peninsula's north side does not extend to the shore as it is blocked by a broad reef. Nonetheless it offers the best-protected harbor in the Marianas. Piti Navy Yard was located at the north end of Apra Harbor. There a 500yd (457m) causeway connects the mainland with 2-mile long Cabras Island, which protects the harbor's north side. Extending west from the island's seaward end is the submerged Luminao Reef on which was built a 1-mile long breakwater. The 4,500ft (1,372m) Orote Airfield had been cleared and staked out, but work had progressed no further.

The value of Guam's exports, mainly copra and coconut oil, totaled a mere sixth of its imports. In 1936, Pan American Airways established a seaplane station at Sumay on the San Francisco–Manila–Hong Kong route. Communications were maintained via the Navy radio station and the Pacific Cable Company had established a commercial telegraph/telephone cable station in 1903.

Agaña, the administrative center, sits on Agaña Bay on the west side of the isthmus with a 1941 population of 12,550. Another 3,000 lived in villages within 10 miles of Agaña and fewer than 3,000 lived in the north. The second largest town was Sumay with 2,000 inhabitants. Numerous villages were scattered about the island, mainly along the coast. Approximately 85 miles (137km) of improved roads served the island. Roads fringed most of the island's southern coast and two crossed the island at the isthmus.

In 1941 the island's population was 23,394: 21,994 Chamorros, 812 non-natives (Americans, Chinese, Japanese), and 588 Navy and Marine personnel including dependents. The official language was English, but the bulk of the population spoke Chamorro at home. The Chamorros, who then preferred to be called Guamanians, were not American citizens, but considered US nationals. This gave them most rights with the exception of voting in US elections.

CHRONOLOGY

1941

17 October US dependents evacuated from Guam.

1 December Emperor gives his approval to attack the US, Commonwealth, and Netherlands.

4 December War warning received by Guam from the Navy Department.

6 December Guam garrison destroys classified documents.

8 December Japanese aircraft attack Guam.

10 December Japanese forces land on Guam and garrison surrenders.

1944

30 January Marines and Army secure Marshall Islands.

17–18 February Navy neutralizes Truk.

22–23 February Navy conducts attacks in southern Marianas.

29 February Army assaults Admiralties.

4 March 29th Division arrives on Guam.

10 March 31st Army established on Saipan to control IJA forces in the Japanese Mandate.

12 March Joint Chiefs of Staff direct that southern Marianas be seized.

20 March Marines secure Emirau. Navy establishes purpose of the Marianas operation. The 6th Expeditionary Force arrives on Guam and is soon reorganized into the 48th Independent Mixed Brigade and 10th Independent Mixed Regiment.

22 March Army assaults Hollandia, New Guinea.

23 March Pacific Fleet issues Marianas operation order.

12 April V Amphibious Corps (VAC) staff split to form Expeditionary Troops and Northern Troops and Landing Force (NTLF) staffs.

23 April Pacific Fleet issues operation plan.

26 April Expeditionary Troops issues operation plan.

11 May Southern Troops and Landing Force (STLF) issues operation plan.

17 May Expeditionary Force issues operation order and sets tentative W-Day as 18 June.

23–27 May Expeditionary Force conducts rehearsals at Guadalcanal.

1–4 June Expeditionary Force departs for Kwajalein.

9–12 June Expeditionary Force departs for Guam.

11–13 June Preparatory naval and air bombardment of Saipan, Tinian, and Guam commences as do air attacks on Rota and Pagan Islands.

15 June (D-Day) 2nd and 4th Marine Divisions (MarDiv) land on Saipan.

16 June W-Day delayed because of approaching Japanese fleet.

19–20 June Battle of the Philippine Sea.

25 June 3rd MarDiv released from NTFL Reserve to STLF and sails to Eniwetok.

26 June Emperor Hirohito requests Foreign Minister to seek peace settlement.

30 June 1st Prov MarBde released from NTLF Reserve to STLF and sales to Kwajalein. W-Day is reset for 25 July then moved up to 21 July.

1 July 77th Infantry Division (InfDiv) departs Hawaii and sails to Eniwetok.

6 July 77th InfDiv released from NTLF Reserve to STLF.

7 July Command of Japanese Tinian forces transferred from Northern Marianas Army Group on Saipan to Southern Marianas Army Group on Guam.

9 July Saipan declared secure.

12 July MajGen Schmidt assumes command of VAC/NTLF to allow LtGen Smith to oversee Guam operation.

15–18 July Southern Attack Force and STLF depart Eniwetok for Guam.

16 July Japanese Government announces Saipan's fall.

A drawing from the *50th Anniversary of the Defense of Guam* booklet depicts two Insular Force Guardsmen, Native Seaman 1st Class (NS1c) Pedro G. Cruz and NS2c Vicente C. Chargualaf, manning a Lewis machine gun on the northwest corner of Plaza de Espana as Japanese SNLF troops entered the square. Defying orders for civilians to remain indoors, 18-year-old Roman E. Camacho helped change magazines. Chargualaf and Camacho were killed in the hour-long fight.

18 July Prime Minister Tojo and cabinet forced to resign.

21 July (W-Day) 3rd MarDiv and 1st Prov MarBde land on Guam.

23–24 July 77th InfDiv lands on Guam.

24 July (J-Day) 4th MarDiv lands on Tinian.

25/26 July Japanese launch major counterattack on Guam and fail.

27 July US sovereignty over Guam proclaimed.

28 July Northern and Southern Beachheads establish firm link-up.

29 July Orote Peninsula secured.

1 August Tinian declared secure.

4 August Orote Airfield operational.

10 August Guam declared secure.

15 September Island Command assumes responsibility for Guam.

1945

24 February First Guam-based B-29 raid on Japan.

6 August Atomic bomb dropped on Hiroshima.

9 August Atomic bomb dropped on Nagasaki.

10 August Japan sues for peace.

14 August Ceasefire in Pacific Theater.

2 September Japan formally surrenders (V-J Day). Japanese forces on Rota and Pagan surrender.

POST-WAR

30 May 1946 US Naval Government re-established.

7 September 1949 Guam transferred from Department of the Navy to Department of the Interior.

1 August 1950 Guamanians received US citizenship.

1962 Naval Clearing Act lifted opening Guam to foreign vessels.

1975 100,000 Vietnamese refugees temporarily housed on Guam.

1996 6,600 Kurdish refugees temporarily housed on Guam.

OPERATION CALENDAR

Guam

X-Day	8 December 1941 (Japan attacks)
X+2	10 December (Japan seizes Guam)

Saipan

D-Day	15 June 1944
D+24	9 July (secured)

Battle of the Philippine Sea

D+4–D+5	19-20 June 1944

Guam		Tinian
W-Day	21 July 1944	
W+1	22 July	
W+2	23 July	
W+3	24 July	J-Day
W+4	25 July	J+1
W+5	26 July	J+2
W+6	27 July	J+3
W+7	28 July	J+4
W+8	29 July	J+5
W+9	30 July	J+6
W+10	31 July	J+7
W+11	1 August	J+8
W+12	2 August	
W+13	3 August	
W+14	4 August	
W+15	5 August	
W+16	6 August	
W+17	7 August	
W+18	8 August	
W+19	9 August	
W+20	10 August	

THE FALL OF GUAM, DECEMBER 1941

"We proclaim herewith that our Japanese Army has occupied Omiya Jima [Great Shrine Island – Guam] by order of the Great Emperor of Japan. It is for the purpose of restoring liberty and rescuing the whole Asiatic people and creating the permanent peace in Asia. Thus our intention is to establish the New Order of the World."

Dated this 10th day of the 12th month of 2601 [1941].
By order of the Japanese Commander-in-Chief.

The fear of war at the beginning of 1941 was especially acute on Guam. In January 1941, by executive order foreign warships and ships of commerce were not permitted to enter the Naval Defense Sea Area and Naval Air Space Reservation 3 miles around Guam and American Samoa; exceptions were granted. Prior to this, Japanese trading schooners routinely visited Guam. In March, Japanese aircraft were detected over-flying the island and it was learned later that these were photo-recon flights. In April plans were announced to expand the naval station and improve the harbor. That same month saw a slight expansion of the Guam Insular Force Guard, a Guamanian-manned militia-type naval station guard. No further efforts were made to fortify the island for fear of complicating ongoing negotiations with Japan. As fear of war increased, 104 American dependents were evacuated to Hawaii and the United States in October aboard the USS *Henderson* followed by over 1,000 construction workers. Further war warnings were issued; Japan's preparations for war were well underway. The Navy had conceded that, if it came to war, Japan would quickly capture Guam.

In December 1941, Naval Forces, Guam, under the command of Captain George J. McMillin, consisted of the Administrative Group, Navy Hospital; Navy Radio Station, Agaña; Navy Radio Station, Libugon (Station B) on Orote Peninsula, and the Navy Yard at Piti, plus the Marine Barracks at Sumay. Naval Forces, Guam was subordinate to the Asiatic Fleet. There were 271 Navy personnel, mostly unarmed, including Guamanian messmen and bandsmen, and four Navy nurses. The USS *Gold Star* (AG-12), Guam's station ship with a 137-man crew, was on a re-supply and Christmas gift buying trip to the Philippines, where it had been ordered to remain.[1]

Marine Barracks, Sumay, Guam had only 153 Marines assigned under Lieutenant Colonel William K. McNulty. This was essentially a company armed with a few .30cal Mk 6 Lewis machine guns, M1918A1 BARs, and M1903 Springfield rifles. There were three Marine-advised militia forces on Guam, all answering to the Governor.

The unarmed and unpaid volunteer Guam Militia was purely a ceremonial marching unit raised in 1917 and played no part in the defense of Guam. However, it served as a training and recruiting ground for the Guam Insular Force Guard. The Guard was established in 1901 to guard

Japanese troops patrolling Agaña. Prior to March 1944 only a few hundred Japanese Navy guard force troops occupied Guam. In the event of difficulties with the Guamanian population, additional troops were to be sent from Saipan.

naval installations. It consisted of 110 men, but in March 1941 was authorized to expand to 234. They received 50 per cent of the pay of an equivalent US Navy rating. By the time of the invasion the Guard had grown to 246 including a 16-man band. They were armed with three Lewis machine guns, four Thompson submachine guns, a few pistols, and 85 Springfield rifles, leaving many men unarmed. The 80-man Guam Insular Patrol, whose personnel were all islanders, was the island's police force and was stationed in villages across the island. It was armed with only .38cal revolvers.

The Japanese Z Operation was planned to commence on 8 December, west of the International Date Line, with the invasions of Malaya, the Philippines, Borneo, Java, Wake, and Guam. Plans were completed in September 1941. The Guam invasion force was the South Seas Detachment (*Nankai Shitai*), aka Horii Force, under Major-General Horii Tomitaro, commanding the 55th Infantry Group. This 4,886-man brigade-size force was drawn from the 55th Division[2] and built around the 144th Infantry Regiment. It was assembled in Korea in November, was sent briefly to Japan and then departed for Chichi Jima in late November. The 370-man 5th Company, *Maizuri* 2nd Special Naval Landing Force (SNLF), based on Saipan, was to be the only unit to engage in combat during the invasion. The 4th Fleet, responsible for the defense of the Japanese Mandated islands, would provide air support with the 22nd Air Flotilla. The South Seas Detachment departed Chichi Jima on 27 November and put in at Haha Jima the next day. It was held there until departing for Guam on 5 December at which time the troops were told their objective.

At 04.45hrs, 8 December (7 December in Hawaii), the Governor was notified of the Pearl Harbor attack. At 08.27hrs IJN aircraft from Saipan attacked the Marine Barracks, Piti Navy Yard, Libugon radio station, Standard Oil Company tank farm (set ablaze), and Pan American Hotel. The 188-ft USS *Penguin* (AM-33) (2 x 3in. guns, 2 x machine-guns) was damaged by bombing off Orote Point and scuttled. One officer was killed and several men wounded including the captain. The immobile 254-ft oil depot ship USS *Robert L. Barnes* (AG-27) was damaged by bombing and strafing. While taking on water, it did not sink and efforts to scuttle it failed. Civilians were evacuated from Agaña and Sumay while some 50 Japanese nationals were arrested and detained in the Agaña jail. The air raids continued all day with the last attack breaking off at 17.00hrs. That night nine Saipan native infiltrators landed by dugout at Ritidian Point on the north end and three were apprehended. Under interrogation they admitted the Japanese were going to land the next morning, but they could only guess where. Captain McMillin suspected that it was a ruse in hopes of the Marines being sent to the island's north end.

At 08.30hrs, 9 December, air attacks resumed with no more than nine aircraft attacking at a time. Attacks were repeated on the previous day's targets plus attempts made to bomb the Government House in Agaña and several villages were strafed resulting in civilian casualties. While

Japanese aircraft were reported shot down, none were. East of the Marine Barracks on Orote Peninsula 122 Marines dug-in at the rifle range along with naval station personnel and some 50 crewmen of the USS *Penguin*. The Guam Insular Force Guard, led by a few Marines, secured government buildings in Agaña. Scattered across the island with the Guam Insular Patrol were a further 28 Marines.

The 370-man 5th Company, *Maizuri* 2nd SNLF landed on Dungcas Beach on Agaña Bay north of Agaña at 02.15hrs, 10 December, and attacked and captured the Insular Force Guard in Agaña. It then advanced on Piti moving toward Sumay and the Marine Barracks. The South Seas Detachment began landing at the same time. Its I Battalion, 144th Infantry (I/144) landed on the north flank of Tumon Bay on the upper northwest coast, north of Dungcas Beach, and moved south toward Agaña. II/144 landed at Talofofo Bay on the lower east coast and moved northwest. The main force of the South Seas Detachment with III/144 landed on the southwest coast near Merizo and moved north to attack the Marines at Sumay with an element going on to Piti Navy Yard.

The principal engagement took place on Agaña's Plaza de Espana, beginning at 04.45hrs, between a few Marines and Insular Force Guardsmen on one side and the SNLF on the other. After token resistance a ceasefire was called at 05.45hrs and the Governor surrendered at 06.00, 10 December, making Guam the first piece of American territory to fall into Japanese hands. The Governor's motivation was to prevent needless deaths among civilians and naval personnel facing overwhelming odds. No fighting occurred at the Marine Barracks, but a few scattered skirmishes took place on the island until word of the surrender spread later in the day. Marine losses were five KIA and 13 WIA. The Navy lost eight KIA and four Guam Insular Force Guards were killed with a total of 22 Navy and Guam Insular Force wounded. About 30 civilians were killed by strafing and bombing along with one American public works civilian. Japanese losses were one dead and six wounded. The few remaining American civilians were interned and later exchanged with diplomatic personnel along with four Navy nurses in June 1942. Six sailors fled to northern Guam. Five were hunted down and killed, but Radioman 1st Class George R. Tweed evaded capture until he was picked up by a destroyer just prior to the 1944 invasion enabling him to provide valuable intelligence information. He was aided by Guamanians who were, as a result, abused and in some cases killed by the Japanese. American military prisoners were held on the island and reasonably treated until shipped to Japan on 10 January 1942. They were later sent to Formosa and then Manchuria as forced labor.

Efforts to prevent useful materiel from falling into Japanese hands were only marginally successful. Of the two yard-patrol craft delivered in October, YP-16 was burned, but YP-17 was damaged and captured. The Japanese later made use of the *Robert L. Barnes* and YP-17. The Marine Barracks' magazine had been destroyed and the Quartermaster stores warehouse and Navy 5,000-barrel fuel oil tank burned. Some 4,000 barrels of PanAm aviation fuel were captured as the burning Standard Oil tank farm prevented efforts to get to the adjacent PanAm tank. Most military and civilian automobiles and trucks on the island were captured, but the heavy trucks left by the Navy construction contractors had been disabled.

The Guamanians suffered heavily under Japanese rule. In addition to changing Guam's name to Omiya Jima (Great Shrine Island), the island's capital of Agaña was renamed Akashi (Bright Red Stone). The Japanese military and civil administration was established at Agaña's Plaza de Espana. Elements of the *Maizuri* 2nd SNLF took over occupation duties. Only Japanese was taught in the schools and rationing was introduced. A Japanese firm, South Seas Development Company, took over all Guamanian business enterprises. Many Guamanians died or otherwise suffered from poor food and limited medicines. Group punishment was inflicted when individuals were accused of infractions of the occupation regulations. The Japanese built two small airfields, a 4,500ft (1,372m) strip on Orote Peninsula and a 5,000ft (1,524m) at Tiyan (aka Agaña) 2 1/2 miles (4km) east of Agaña, which was not quite completed by the time of the 1944 invasion. An airstrip was cleared, but no other work completed, at Dededo 3 miles (4.8km) northeast of Tiyan and near Tumon Bay on the west coast. Sumay on Orote Peninsula was off-limits to Guamanians, as was the entire peninsula. Guamanians, including women and children, were forced to help with airfield construction, along with building fortifications. The Japanese performed little other military construction on the island, only exploiting its resources. When reinforcements began to arrive on the island in March 1944, the schools and churches were closed, more restrictive rationing imposed, punishments became harsher, and more civilians were impressed into forced labor. Their deliverance was not now long in coming.

The South Seas Detachment departed Guam on 14 January 1942 to occupy Rabaul, New Britain, on 23 January. The 144th was responsible for the murder of 150 Australian prisoners on New Britain. In March II/144 landed at Salamaua, north-east New Guinea. In May, I/144 was sent to occupy Port Moresby, Papua New Guinea, but turned back during the battle of the Coral Sea. The 144th was sent to Buna and virtually destroyed in August. The survivors were withdrawn; the unit was rebuilt, and rejoined the 55th Division in Burma.

---

1 Ordered to Australia, it survived the war serving as a coastal cargo ship until 1946.
2 The rest of the 55th Division was deployed to Indochina and fought in Burma until the war's end.

THE RECAPTURE AND OCCUPATION OF GUAM, 1944

OPPOSING PLANS

THE AMERICAN PLAN – OPERATION FORAGER

Marine V Amphibious Corps (VAC) was assigned responsibility for Operation "Forager", the US assault on the Marianas, on 15 January 1944. The tempo of Allied operations increased markedly following the neutralization of Truk and, on 13 March, Admiral Nimitz gave orders that Forager's planning be given the highest priority.

The Japanese defense of the Marianas focused on the five largest islands, which were held in strength. Saipan, the second largest island, was the main Japanese stronghold and the US Command decided this would be assaulted first on 15 June, with Tinian to follow on an unspecified date. The assault on Guam (W-Day[3]) was provisionally set for 18 June, but the actual date would be finalized based on the tactical situation. It was decided to bypass the islands of Rota and Pagan.

Prior to seizing Guam (code-named "Stevedore"), VAC would secure Saipan and begin construction of the B-29 airbases as early as possible. To seize Guam, III Amphibious Corps (IIIAC)[4] was assigned the 3rd Marine Division (MarDiv), 1st Provisional Marine Brigade (Prov MarBde), 77th Infantry Division (InfDiv), and IIIAC Artillery. VAC was designated the Northern Troops and Landing Force (NTLF) while IIIAC was the Southern Troops and Landing Force (STLF). Lieutenant General Holland M. Smith, Commanding General, VAC, was designated Commanding General, Expeditionary Troops with authority over both NTLF and STLF.

Planning guides were prepared by higher headquarters and provided to IMAC (IIIAC) on 30 March. The Corps submitted a tentative plan on 3 April, which was approved by LtGen Smith and then the navy commanders. IMAC was headquartered on Guadalcanal at the time, as was the 3rd MarDiv. The 1st Prov MarBde was in the process of forming and its subordinate units would be transferred to Guadalcanal to allow planning, training, and rehearsals with the Corps. Expeditionary Troops and VAC were in Hawaii. The staff of the Southern Attack Force (Task Force TF 53), the naval force that would deliver and support STLF, arrived at Guadalcanal to expedite planning and coordination on 15 April. Most of the ships that would comprise TF 53 were still off New Guinea where

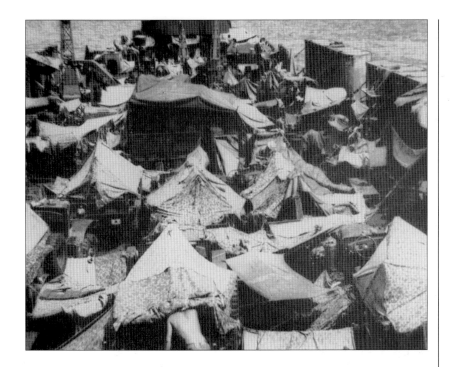

Marines en route to Guam on a landing ship tank, (LST), or "large slow target," camped out on the deck to avoid the ship's sweltering interior. Camouflage shelter halves ("pup tents"), ponchos, and canvas traps give the deck the appearance of a floating hobo camp.

they had supported the Hollandia landing. Most had arrived in the Solomons in May for repairs and replenishing.

"Forager" was a complex operation with two major landing forces tasked with securing three different islands. It was foreseen the Guam assault would probably be delayed depending on developments on Saipan. NTLF would initially be the lead force. Its success on Saipan would dictate all subsequent operations along with the employment of the reserve and STLF with the latter also serving as a reserve for the NTLF until 25 June. The 77th InfDiv initially remained in Hawaii as the Area Reserve.

In the intelligence arena the capture of 31st Army documents on Saipan provided a great deal of information on Japanese forces on Guam. In late May the US estimate of Japanese strength on Guam was 10,100–11,800. On 18 July this was revised to 18,657 Imperial Japanese Army and Navy personnel.

A unique aspect of the STLF plan was that the two landing forces would be separated by almost 7 miles (11km). It was unprecedented for two landing forces to land with such a wide separation. The Army had recently landed two divisions at Hollandia on New Guinea separated by 25 miles, but for all practical purposes these were two separate operations. There was no expectation for early link-up and the goal was to entrap the Japanese in a double-envelopment. It also allowed for one of the forces being delayed by enemy action or difficult terrain. The calculated risk taken on Guam was justifiable because of the location of suitable landing beaches and the fact that the bulk of the Japanese forces were positioned at and between the two beaches. This risk was necessary because they were the only suitable beaches on the cliff-lined island. One of the landing's key initial goals, besides establishing forces ashore and inflicting an early beating on the main defending forces, was to secure Apra Harbor. The northern force would secure the immediate harbor area while the southern force cleared the dominating Orote Peninsula, control of which was vital to allow use of the harbor.

The 3rd MarDiv would land on the Northern or Asan Beaches situated between Adelup and Asan Points, both Japanese strongpoints. These beaches totaled only about 2,500 yards (2286m) in width. Asan Town was dead in the center of the beaches. All three regiments would land abreast, with only 1/9 Marines serving as a Reserve as the Division relied on the Corps Reserve. Overlooking the beaches was Bundschu Ridge[5] on the edge of Fonte Plateau. The 3rd Marines would secure Adelup Point and seize Bundschu Ridge. The 21st Marines in the center would push inland up the two branches of the Asan River. The 9th Marines would seize Asan Point and push toward Apra Harbor.

The 1st Prov MarBde would assault the Southern or Agat Beaches. These were in Agat Bay south of Orote Peninsula and overlooked by the 869ft (265m) Mt. Alifan. The rice paddies behind the beaches disappeared as the ground rose towards Mt. Alifan. The 22nd Marines would swing north toward Orote Peninsula. The 4th Marines would both secure the south flank on Bangi Point and block Harmon Road. The 4th Marines would be followed ashore by the 305th Infantry landing on order. The 305th would takeover the defense of the Force Beachhead Line (FBL) from the Brigade, secure the high ground above the beaches, and extend the beachhead south. The Brigade would then make a concerted effort to seize Orote Peninsula. IIIAC Artillery would land on the Southern Beaches to provide fire support to the north.

The remainder of the 77th InfDiv initially served as the STLF Reserve. The Expeditionary Troops Floating Reserve was the 26th Marines (Reinforced) with 1/13 Marines [artillery], detached from the 5th MarDiv still in the States. The latter was sent to Hawaii at the end of July as it was not needed.

IIIAC conducted training and rehearsals at Guadalcanal, but the 77th InfDiv, still in Hawaii, could not take part. On 1 June units began departing for Kwajalein, and then on to the Saipan area on the 12th arriving on the 16th. They remained there until the 25th at which time the 3rd MarDiv was

Artillerymen of Howitzer Battalion, 22nd Marines, 1st Prov MarBde, are briefed on a Guam terrain board by the Bn-2 (intelligence officer) while en route to Guam. He is pointing to the Southern Beaches where they will follow their regiment ashore.

sent to Eniwetok. The 1st Prov MarBde remained on station until the 30th and then returned to Kwajalein.

While the assault on Guam was tentatively scheduled for 18 June, it was delayed by over a month for several reasons. It was discovered that the 1st Mobile Fleet was approaching the Marianas from the Philippines at that time and the landing was postponed so as not to endanger the Southern Attack Force en route to Guam. With the battle of the Philippine Sea over, another delay was imposed because of the stronger than expected resistance on Saipan. This required that the Expeditionary Troops Reserve, the 27th InfDiv, be committed. Fearing additional reinforcement might be required on Saipan; the 1st Prov MarBde was retained in the area as the Expeditionary Troops Reserve.

In the meantime it was decided to release the General Reserve at Hawaii, the 77th InfDiv, to the STLF on 6 July for use on Guam. The entire division could not deploy immediately because the necessary transports were still at Saipan. However, on 30 June it was decided the landing should not be attempted until the entire 77th was on-station. W-Day was reset for 25 July. When it was learned that the Division would be assembled at Eniwetok in its entirety by the 18th, W-Day was moved forward to 21 July.

THE JAPANESE DEFENSE PLAN

Following the loss of most of eastern New Guinea and the Solomon Islands, in September 1943 the Imperial General Headquarters established the National Defense Zone, known to the Allies as the "Tojo Line". With the capture of Kwajalein in February, the Imperial Japanese Navy expected an assault on the Marianas by the end of March. By April the Admiralty Islands had fallen, and both Truk and the Marshalls had been neutralized. The IJN belief, reinforced by the continued advance westward of MacArthur's forces along the north New Guinea coast, was that the next strike would be in the Palaus or elsewhere in the Western Carolines. Although the Imperial Japanese Army made some efforts to reinforce the Marianas in March, it would be May before the bulk of the units arrived; less than two months before the invasion. In June orders were issued (but never executed) for some IJA personnel to transfer from the Marianas to the Palaus; a result of the IJA conviction that the Palaus were now the most likely target of an American attack

The Imperial General Headquarters issued plans for Operation *A-Go* on 3 May 1944, and the Combined Fleet prepared to face the invading US Fleet in a decisive engagement in the Palaus-Carolines area. In this it would be supported by land-based IJN and IJA aircraft in the Philippines, Carolines, Palaus, and Marianas, and in June more than 500 additional land-based aircraft deployed to the Mandate. After it withdrew from Truk, the Combined Fleet was based at Tawitawi Island off the northeast tip of Borneo, allowing it to sail south of the Philippines or direct to the Palaus or Western Carolines. The southern Marianas were some considerable distance further from Tawitawi, however, and fuel was in short supply.

The US had carried out no major operations in the Central Pacific since February, and by the beginning of June Imperial General Headquarters was expecting some move in this theater. However, on 27 May MacArthur's forces had landed on Biak, only 800 miles (1,288km) from

the southern Philippines and it was possible this might now be the main Allied thrust. As a result many of Guam's aircraft were sent to Biak, and few returned.

Before 10 March 1944 the 4th Fleet had been solely responsible for the defense of the Mandates, but on this date IJN established the Central Pacific Area Fleet. This new command oversaw the Volcano and Bonin Islands, Marianas, and Western Carolines and 4th Fleet was subordinate to it, retaining direct control over Truk, the Eastern Carolines, and those islands in the Marshalls bypassed by the Allied advance. In theory, the Central Pacific Area Fleet was also to have control of IJA units in the area, but 31st Army, headquartered on Saipan, refused subordination to the IJN. In mid-March a dreadful compromise solution was reached by which each island was commanded by the senior IJA or IJN commander present. Neither 31st Army or Central Pacific Area Fleet would assume overall authority of the area, with the result that there was no unified Japanese command in the Central Pacific.

In previous US assaults on islands in the Central Pacific Theater, the Japanese had defended the beaches, intending to destroy the landing force at the water's edge. These had, however, mainly been very small atoll islands with no space for multiple lines of defense or reserves to maneuver and artillery placed on the shoreline. An airfield often occupied the bulk of the island, and there were seldom the dominating terrain features necessary to establish in-depth defenses.

The hilly islands of the Marianas were considerably larger allowing the creation of multiple lines of defense. Although strongpoints could be sited on key terrain features, and there was sufficient room for reserves to maneuver and counterattack, the Japanese proved unable to capitalize on these various advantages.

The IJN 54th Guard Force with its coast defense and antiaircraft guns was able to encase many in reinforced concrete positions, but other positions were uncompleted. Sizable IJA forces had arrived in March giving them over four months to prepare. One final advantage enjoyed by Guam's Japanese defenders was an additional 35 days after the Saipan attack began to prepare for the inevitable assault. This was somewhat negated by the paucity of construction materials.

Many Japanese units had suffered heavily from the attentions of the US submarine force even before they reached the islands, losing weapons, essential equipment, and much of their unit cohesion. This was particularly true of the 29th Division: its 18th Infantry had lost many troops and most of its equipment. Although the regiment was partly rebuilt, its 50th Infantry ended up on Tinian and an additional battalion was diverted to Saipan. On its arrival, all IJN units on Guam were placed under 29th Division control, which doubled as the Southern Marianas Army Group and, in this capacity, was also responsible for Rota.

I/10 Independent Mixed Regiment (IMR) was deployed to Rota. A few days later III/18 Infantry followed to provide amphibious reinforcement for Guam. Rough seas, which led to the loss of 100 men and two landing barges, and the high probability that the force would be interdicted, resulted in the battalion being returned to Guam for more practical employment. Time for preparations was running out and the Japanese concentrated on fortifying the high ground overlooking the most likely landing beaches. The landward neck of Orote Peninsula was heavily

fortified, but this succeeded only in effectively trapping the defenders. Although they delayed the Americans making Apra Harbor operational, this was outweighed by their inability to contribute to the prolonged defense of the island. Small dumps of ammunition, rations, and medical supplies were positioned all over the island.

Lieutenant-General Takeshi, commanding the 29th Division and Southern Marianas Army Group, established specific defense sectors. The 48th Independent Mixed Brigade (IMB) was assigned to defend the Asan Beaches, with both the 10th IMR and the 29th Division's 18th Infantry (-) attached in support. The Brigade's 320th IIB was on the plateau overlooking the Asan Beaches, 321st IIB defended northern Agaña Bay, including Dungcas Beach where the SNLF had come ashore in 1941, and the 322nd IIB secured Tumon Bay further to the north. The 2nd Company, 9th Tank Regiment (2/9 Tank) backed the Brigade at Sinajana. The 48th IMB's Artillery Unit was scattered across the Agaña area with some guns positioned inland. The 18th Infantry (-) retained control of only its III Battalion defending the harbor. The 38th Infantry was responsible for the Agat Beaches. I/38 Infantry defended the southern portion of Agat Bay and II/38 the northern. Elements of the 54th Guard Force defended the Orote Peninsula along with the 800-man *Hyo* Unit and the 700-man *Genzan* Unit formed from the IJN 263rd and 755th Air Groups, respectively. Commander Tamai Asaichi of the 263rd Air Group was responsible for the peninsula's defense and controlled II/38 at its neck. A mobile reserve was held under the 29th Division behind Fonte Plateau comprised of III/38 Infantry, 319th IIB; 9th Company, III/38 IMR; and 24th Tank Company plus the 400-man *Otori* Unit, made up of IJN 521st Air Group personnel. The southern end of the island was defended by the 10th IMR. Its III/10 was on the south end spread out between Umatac and Inarajan while II/10 was between Pago and Ylig Bays. II/18 Infantry was at Finaguayac on Guam's north end.

Regardless of efforts at deception made by the Americans to bombard beaches other than the actual landing sites, the Japanese command was

Guam was flailed with the longest pre-landing bombardment to date. Orote Peninsula especially was blasted, as it was known to be a Japanese strongpoint covering the Southern Beaches and Apra Harbor to the north. The Marines aimed to capture the peninsula as early as possible to allow the 3rd MarDiv and 1st Prov MarBde to link-up, and to capture, repair and use its airfield. The white strip of the airfield can be seen in the center. Cabras Island on the north side of Apra Harbor is in the upper right.

able to identify Asan and Agat Beaches as the most likely targets. Beginning on 8 July the 10th IMR began withdrawing its two battalions from the south of the island and assembled them at Ordat. 9th Company, III/10 IMR was placed in a reserve position near Mt. Alifan to support the 38th Infantry. II/18 Infantry in the north also assembled at Ordat to reinforce the Asan Beaches. The 322nd IIB remained at Tumon Bay.

With shortages of small arms and infantry crew-served weapons for the ad hoc rifle units, little medium artillery, low supplies of AA ammunition, and no hope of air support or reinforcement, the Japanese tactical defense situation was bleak. In addition to relying on the ability of the Combined Fleet to defeat the American invasion fleet, the *A-Go* Operation counted on land-based aircraft to launch attacks and provide air cover. A total of 14 airfields and two seaplane bases were supposed to be completed in the Marianas by April. Although the seaplane bases were finished, only nine of the airfields were operational. The operational fields could support 400 aircraft, but American air attacks and naval bombardment destroyed all aircraft prior to Saipan's D-Day. Guam's 80 fighters and 80 bombers were destroyed on or over the island itself or lost supporting the defense of Biak.

---

3 Each island was assigned a different letter identifying its assault date to prevent confusion between operations; D-Day for Saipan, J-Day for Tinian, and W-Day for Guam.
4 At the time the assignments were made, IIIAC was designated I Marine Amphibious Corps (IMAC). It was redesignated IIIAC on 15 April 1944.
5 The ridge was named after Captain Geary R. Bundschu commanding A/1/3, who was killed leading his unit to capture the feature.

OPPOSING COMMANDERS

AMERICAN COMMANDERS

Captain George J. McMillin (US Navy) (misspelled McMillan in many references) joined the Navy in 1907 from Ohio and graduated from the Naval Academy in 1911. He attended the Naval War College and accumulated over 16 years of sea duty aboard carriers, battleships, cruisers, and destroyers. Additionally, he was credited with Mexican, Dominican Republic, and World War I sea service. McMillin also served at the Navy Department, Naval Academy, and Naval War College. He was assigned as Governor of Guam and Commandant of Naval Station, Guam on 20 April 1940. After surrendering Guam in December 1941, he was confined in Japan, Formosa, and Manchuria for almost three years. He was assigned as Chief of Staff, Naval Base, Long Beach, California, retiring as a rear admiral in 1949. He served as the Postmaster of the City of Long Beach until 1961 and died in 1983.

Vice Admiral Richmond K. Turner (US Navy) graduated from the Naval Academy in 1908 and during World War I he served aboard battleships. In 1926, however, he made a major career change and was rated a Naval Aviator. He subsequently held a series of aviation staff positions, including executive officer of an aircraft carrier, finally being appointed Commander, Aircraft, Battle Force of the US Fleet. Following a period commanding a cruiser, he attended the Naval War College and at the beginning of the war he was Director of the Navy Department's War Plans Division. Turner took command of South Pacific amphibious forces

Left to right: MajGen Henry L. Larsen (Commanding General, Island Command, Guam), MajGen Roy S. Geiger (Commanding General, IIIAC/STLF), LtGen Holland M. Smith (Commanding General, Expeditionary Troops and FMF, Pacific), and LtGen Alexander A. Vandergrift (Commandant of the Marine Corps) during the 10 August High Command inspection when Guam was declared secure.

Left to right: BrigGen Alfred H. Noble (Assistant Division Commander, 3rd MarDiv), Capt Pat Buchanan (Commander, Northern Transport Group), RearAdm Richard L. Conolly (Commander, Southern Attack Force and Northern Attack Group), and MajGen Allen H. Turnage (Commanding General, 3rd MarDiv).

in the summer of 1942, where his previous experience served him well in the grueling Solomons campaign, although he did suffer his only defeat during the battle of Savo Island. He was given command of Fifth Fleet Amphibious Force in August 1943, to perfect landing force operations for the Gilberts and Marshalls operations. At Saipan and Tinian he commanded both the Joint Expeditionary Force and the Northern Attack Force, and then oversaw the landings on Guam and Okinawa, directing all amphibious forces of the Third and Fifth Fleets. Turner was the US Navy representative to the UN Military Staff Committee after the war until he retired in 1947. Admiral Turner died in 1961.

Lieutenant General Holland M. Smith (USMC) was commissioned in the Marine Corps in 1905, but had previously been a practicing Alabama lawyer. He served in France in World War I, and previously in the Philippines, Panama and the Dominican Republic. It was in the latter that he received his appropriate nickname, "Howlin' Mad". Graduating from the War College in 1921, experience gained in a series of subsequent posts within the Marine Corps allowed him to create, in the Fleet Marine Force (FMF), a first-rate amphibious assault force. Made commander of 1st Marine Brigade in 1939, it was expanded into the 1st Marine Division in 1941. He quickly assumed command of Amphibious Force, Atlantic Fleet and then Amphibious Corps, Pacific Fleet, redesignated VAC in August 1942. Promoted to lieutenant general in May 1944, Smith oversaw the capture of Tarawa, Makin, Roi-Namur, Kwajalein, and Eniwetok in his capacity as VAC commander, and was designated Commanding General, Expeditionary Troops for the Marianas campaign. In July 1944, Smith took command of the newly activated FMF, Pacific to oversee all Marine forces in the Pacific, having relinquished command of VAC. A highly controversial character, Smith put great strain on Army/Marine Corps relations by relieving Major General Ralph C. Smith of his command of 27th Infantry Division. His scathing criticism of the Army and Navy eventually became a liability to joint operations and Smith was replaced as commander of FMFPac in July 1945 by LtGen Roy S. Geiger. Retiring in 1946 Smith died in 1967.

Major General Roy S. Geiger (USMC) was considered an oddity by many – he was a Naval Aviator, the fifth Marine to become a pilot, and an amphibious corps commander. He flew in and commanded Marine aviation units from 1917 right up to assuming command of IMAC in November 1943. Geiger enlisted in the Marine Corps in 1907 after graduating from college. He was commissioned an infantry officer two

MajGen Andrew D. Bruce (right), Commanding General, 77th InfDiv with Col Douglas C. McNair, his Chief of Staff. A sniper killed McNair on 6 August. His father, LtGen Leslie J. McNair (Commanding General, Army Ground Forces), was killed by inaccurate US bombs at St Lô, France, 12 days earlier.

years later to serve in Central America, China, and elsewhere. Between major aviation commands, he attended the Army's Command and General Staff School and War College, and then the Naval War College. In August 1941, Geiger took command of the 1st Marine Aircraft Wing taking it to Guadalcanal where he was promoted to major general. In May 1943 he was assigned as Director, Division of Aviation, Headquarters, Marine Corps. In November, he took command of IMAC, considered an unusual move by many due to his flying vocation. He excelled in two areas critical to successful corps operations, however, fire support (artillery, naval, air) and logistics. He led the Corps on Bougainville then Guam (the Corps was redesignated IIIAC in April 1944). He then took it to Peleliu and Okinawa. With the death of LtGen Buckner on 18 June 1945, Geiger assumed command of Tenth Army, the only Marine officer to command a field army, while retaining command of IIIAC. The next day, he was promoted to lieutenant general. Five days later, Geiger was relieved with the arrival of LtGen Joseph W. Stilwell. In July 1945, Geiger took command of FMFPac, and in late 1946 was assigned to Headquarters, Marine Corps, but became ill just before his scheduled retirement and died in January 1947. Later in the year, a grateful Congress gave him a posthumous promotion to full general.

Major General Allen H. Turnage (USMC) was commissioned in the Marine Corps in 1913. He served in Haiti from 1915 to 1918 and again from 1922 to 1925. In between these tours he fought in France in 1918 and was an instructor at Marine Corps Schools. He later served in sea assignments and in 1935 was director of The Basic School. He served in China from 1939 to 1941 and was then Director of the Division of Plans and Policies. He commanded Camp Lejeune, North Carolina, in 1942 after promotion to brigadier general, where he oversaw the training of two Marine regiments that would be assigned to the 3rd MarDiv. He took command of 3rd MarDiv in September 1943, having previously

LtGen Takeshi Takahina commanded the 29th Division and doubled as the Southern Marianas Army Group commander until killed when withdrawing from Fonte Plateau on 28 July after the ill-fated 25/26 July counterattack.

LtGen Obata Hideyoshi, commanding the 31st Army, was conducting an inspection in the Palaus when the Americans struck Saipan, his headquarters. He made his way to Guam where he established a new headquarters. He assumed direct command of forces on Guam after the death of the 29th Division commander on 28 July.

been the unit's assistant commander, and led the Division during the 1½-month long Bougainville operation in late 1943. After Guam he became the Director of Personnel and in 1945 the Assistant Commandant of the Marine Corps followed by Commanding General, FMFPac. He was promoted to full general upon retirement in 1948 and passed away in 1977.

Brigadier General Lemuel C. Shepard, Jr. (USMC) was commissioned in the Marine Corps before graduating from the Virginia Military Institute in 1917 to serve in France where he saw a great deal of action. Between the wars he served in China and Haiti and also held a number of command, staff, and training assignments. He commanded the 9th Marines and deployed it to the Pacific with the 3rd MarDiv from 1942–43. He became the assistant division commander of the 1st MarDiv in mid-1943, participating in the two-month Cape Gloucester, New Britain, campaign in early 1944. There he formed the Assistant Division Commander Group, built around the 7th Marines, which operated as a brigade semi-independent of the Division. In April he assumed command of the new 1st Prov MarBde leading it to Guam. He became the commanding general of the 6th MarDiv when the Brigade formed its core in September and commanded it until late 1946, during which time the Division occupied North China. He subsequently served as Assistant Commandant of the Marine Corps; Commanding General, FMFPac; and Commandant from 1952–56 when he retired as a full general. He died in 1990.

Major General Andrew D. Bruce (USA), from Missouri, was commissioned in 1917 from Texas A&M. He served in France in the 2nd Division alongside Marines. Numerous staff and command assignments followed between the wars as well as attending the Command and General Staff School, Army War College, and Naval War College. America's entry into the war saw him commanding the Tank Destroyer School. He took command of the 77th Infantry Division in May 1943, a post he retained until 1946 leading it through Guam, Leyte, and Okinawa. After the war he commanded the 7th Infantry Division, was deputy commander of Fourth Army, and commandant of the Armed Forces Staff College. He retired as a lieutenant general in 1954 and died in 1969.

JAPANESE COMMANDERS

Major-General Horii Tomitaro (IJA) was commissioned an infantry sub-lieutenant in 1911. He held numerous infantry command and training assignments reaching battalion commander in 1932 and regimental commander in 1938. Horii served at least one tour in China and was promoted to major-general in 1939. As the commander of the 55th Infantry Group, 55th Division, he formed the South Seas Detachment in November 1941. He seized Guam and then Rabaul, where his troops murdered 200 Australian captives. He accompanied I Battalion, 144th Infantry in the attempted Port Moresby landing, but the invasion convoy turned back during the battle of the Coral Sea. He later fought in northeast New Guinea suffering repeated defeats at the hands of US and Australian forces. In November 1942 he drowned attempting to cross the Kumusi River while fleeing Australian troops after his defeat at the battle of Oivi.

Lieutenant-General Takeshi Takahina (IJA) Virtually nothing is known of this officer's career other than that he served in Manchuria with the 29th Division before it deployed to Guam in 1944. There he commanded both the 29th Division and Southern Marianas Army Group. Takeshi ordered a futile *banzai* counterattack on 25 July and was killed by US tank machine gun fire on the 28th while directing the withdrawal from Fonte Plateau.

Major-General Shigematsu Kiyoshi (IJA) is another officer of whom little is known. He arrived on Guam in March 1944 in command of the 6th Expeditionary Unit. It was split and reorganized as the 10th IMR and 48th IMB with Shigematsu taking command of the latter formation. Shigematsu was formerly the 11th Infantry Group commander of the 11th Division stationed in Manchuria. He was killed by tank gunfire on 26 July at his Mt. Mangan command post after the failed counterattack.

Lieutenant-General Obata Hideyoshi (IJA) (also listed Obata Eiryo), commanding the 31st Army, was caught in the Palaus on an inspection trip when the American Expeditionary Force arrived at Saipan. His plans and preparations had some affect on the battle. Obata had graduated from the Army War College in 1919 after being commissioned in the cavalry in 1911. He was a military student in Britain in the 1920s and held a number of staff, instructor, and cavalry command assignments. In 1935 he went into aviation and commanded various air units. His 5th Air Group attacked the Philippines on 9 December 1941 and was soon fighting in Burma. He later commanded the 3rd Air Army and was then on the Army General Staff. He took command of the 31st Army in March 1944 with responsibility for the defense of the Mariana, Marshall, Caroline, Palau, Bonin, and Volcano Islands. It was envisioned that the defense of the islands would be largely conducted by air units. He was able to make it to Guam from the Palaus and established a new skeleton headquarters. He still had authority over Saipan and Tinian, but was able to have little direct impact on the battle. Obata's presence on Guam was initially unknown to the American command. With the death of the 29th Division commander on 28 July, Obata took direct command of forces on Guam. He committed suicide on 11 August as US troops overran his Mt. Mataguac command post and was later posthumously promoted to full general.

Captain Sugimoto Yutaka (IJN), the senior Japanese naval officer on Guam, commanded the 54th Guard Force and the air service units. Nothing is known of this officer. It appears he cooperated with the IJA commander maneuvering his units as directed. This may have been due to a realization of the seriousness of the situation after more strongly defended Saipan's fall. He may have died in the Mt. Santa Rosa area in the last days of the battle, but could also have perished during or immediately after the 25/26 July counterattack.

OPPOSING FORCES

US FORCES –
JOINT EXPEDITIONARY FORCE

The entire Marianas operation was controlled by Vice Adm Turner's **Joint Expeditionary Force** (Task Force 51), which was itself subordinate to the **Fifth Fleet and Central Pacific Forces** (TF 50) under Vice Adm Raymond A. Spruance. Both **Fast Carrier Force** (TF 58), under Vice Adm Marc A. Mitschner, and Vice Adm John H. Hover's **Forward Area, Central Pacific** (TF 57), controlling land-based aircraft, came under Spruance's authority and supported the Marianas operation. TF 58 had 15 carriers with 900 aircraft while TF 57 included the Fifth, Seventh and Thirteenth Air Forces and 4th Marine Aircraft Wing.

Task Force 51 included **Northern Attack Force** (TF 52) for Saipan and Tinian, **Southern Attack Force** (TF 53) for Guam, and **Expeditionary Troops** (TF 56). Three task groups provided reserves and garrison forces: Joint Expeditionary Reserve (TG 51.1) with 27th InfDiv (afloat), Defense and Garrison Groups (Task Group 52.2 to 51.7), General Reserve (TG 51.8) with 77th InfDiv (Hawaii), and Landing Craft, Tank Flotilla 13 (TG 51.9).

The Expeditionary Troops were split into two separate task groups. Northern Troops and Landing Force (NTLF) (TG 56.1), whose target was

Beaches "Green" and "Blue" on the Northern Beaches on which the 3rd MarDiv's 22nd and 9th Marines landed respectively. Asan Point is in the lower right of the photo. The dip in the shoreline is the mouth of the Asan River. Asan Village is to the left of the river's mouth. The open rice paddies the Marines had to cross to reach the defended ridges dominating the beaches give an appreciation of the advantage the Japanese held.

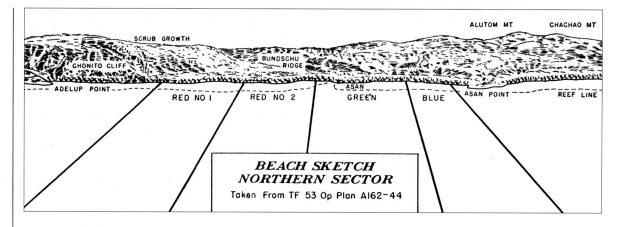

BEACH SKETCH
NORTHERN SECTOR
Taken From TF 53 Op Plan A162-44

Saipan, and Southern Troops and Landing Force (NTLF) (TG 56.2) with IIIAC for Guam. Although the Japanese defenders of Guam numbered only about half those on Saipan, based on the necessity of committing the 27th InfDiv to Saipan, STLF was reinforced with the 77th InfDiv.

At Tetera, Guadalcanal, the 3rd MarDiv conducted extensive training with amtracs and experimented with the most effective ways of crossing reefs. The landings on Bougainville, their previous operation, had been effected solely with landing craft. The unit also tested landing tanks and bringing artillery ashore in the new DUKW ("Duck") amphibious trucks.

At Tassafaronga, Guadalcanal, the newly formed 1st Prov MarBde was trying to rapidly shape itself into a combined arms force. Its two formerly separate reinforced infantry regiments arrived in late April. To save time they remained organized as regimental combat teams. The 4th Marines, organized from the former raider battalions, arrived from its unopposed occupation of Emirau while the 22nd Marines came from Kwajalein after seizing Eniwetok. The 4th Marines had never used amtracs and the 22nd had minimal experience with Army amtracs at Eniwetok. The Division and the Brigade conducted extensive tank-infantry team training and tankers were trained as artillery forward observers allowing them to call for fire support directly from the frontline. The hastily assembled and inadequately manned staff hampered the Brigade. Some 1,800 troops of the 22nd were afflicted with slow-manifesting filariasis (aka elephantiasis) contracted while in the Samoas in 1943. Surplus troops from 3rd MarDiv and replacements from the United States took their places, greatly reducing the number of experienced leaders and troops and requiring an intensified training program.

Between 12 and 22 May a full-range of landing exercises were conducted at Cape Esperance, followed by complete rehearsals on 23–24 May. The troops had undergone effective training, units were slightly over-strength and morale was high. However, the average 50 days spent afloat since departing Guadalcanal would begin to take the edge off the Marines.

Although previously employed on Saipan, several weapons new to the Marines were fielded. IIIAC had only one platoon of the truck-mounted 4.5in. Mk 7 multiple rocket launcher, and only the 3rd MarDiv had any flamethrower tanks – six M4A2 Shermans fitted with E4-5 flameguns in lieu of the bow machine guns. The supporting amtracs were mostly the old LVT(2) with few rear ramp-equipped LVT(4)s available. No 75mm howitzer-armed LVT(A)4 amphibian tanks were available, only the

37mm LVT(A)1. The 22nd Marines had arrived on Guadalcanal without bazookas, but the Army was able to supply them. In their first use in the Pacific, the 77th InfDiv deployed with 3in. gun-armed M10 tank destroyers in lieu of 57mm towed AT guns.

US Marine Corps

III Amphibious Corps had originated as I Marine Amphibious Corps on 1 October 1942 at San Diego, California. It initially served as an operational headquarters for all Marine forces in the South Pacific to control Marine operations on Guadalcanal, Russell Islands, New Georgia, and Bougainville into 1944. It was on Guadalcanal when it was assigned the Guam mission. On 15 April 1944 IMAC was redesignated IIIAC. IIIAC Service Group would take over the shore parties and oversee the development of the port and airbases on Guam. The 5th Field Depot provided logistical support. A total of 6,719 troops manned Corps Troops and IIIAC Artillery.

The **3rd Marine Division** was organized from several existing separate regiments on 16 September 1942 at Camp Elliott, California. At the time of its activation some of its units were on the East Coast. Its 3rd Marines was serving in Samoa and did not join the Division until after it had arrived in New Zealand in early 1943. "The Fighting Third" moved to Guadalcanal between June and August and assaulted Bougainville at the end of the year. It returned to Guadalcanal in January 1944 and was scheduled to assault New Ireland, but this operation was cancelled and the 3rd MarDiv was designated for Guam. The Division would assault with 20,338 troops.

The **1st Provisional Marine Brigade** was formed on Guadalcanal on 19 April 1944. Its staff had been activated on Hawaii on 22 March and arrived on Guadalcanal on 22 April, at the same time as its two regiments. The unit trained quickly and was sent to the Saipan area to serve as the VAC Floating Reserve until released back to IIIAC to prepare for Guam. The Brigade would land with 9,886 troops, not including the approximately 4,500 men of the attached 305th Infantry.

A view from Fonte Plateau near the beachhead's north end. Landing ships and craft can be seen lining the "Red" Beaches at the upper left.

The lead assault waves of the 1st Prov MarBde approach the Southern Beaches on W-Day. Smoke from fires began by the intense bombardment are apparent. Receiving an especially heavy pounding is Apaca Point near the neck of the Orote Peninsula. The 4th Marines' "White" Beaches are at the bottom of the photo and the 22nd Marines' "Yellow" Beaches are in the shallow indentation in the shoreline immediately above them.

Once the island was secure the 3rd MarDiv would be turned over to Island Command, Guam, which would oversee the mopping-up of the island, defense, security, and base development. IIIAC Service Group would become subordinate to Island Command. The 5th Naval Construction Brigade would begin building airfields and support facilities.

In the Saipan operation the Marine divisions were augmented by Army amphibian tractor battalions and various small support units; this was not the case on Guam where most support came from Marine assets.

The Marine infantry regiments committed to this operation were the 3rd, 9th, 21st (3rd MarDiv); 4th, 22nd (1st Prov MarBde). 12th Marines was the 3rd MarDiv's artillery regiment and 19th Marines its engineers.

In the reorganization of the Marine divisions carried out in early 1944, the artillery regiment was reduced to four battalions, the special weapons battalion eliminated, and the amphibian tractor battalion reassigned to FMF. As they were integrated into the unit's plan, 3rd MarDiv retained its engineer regiment, although this unit had in theory been eliminated as part of the reorganization.

Marine tank battalions' M3A1 light tanks gave way to the more powerful M4A2 Sherman medium tanks. Each company had 15 Shermans armed with the 75mm gun. In addition the headquarters battalion absorbed the reconnaissance company from each of the tank battalions.

1st and 2nd Battalions, 12th Marines [artillery], had 75mm M1A1 pack howitzers and 3rd and 4th Battalions, the 105mm M2A1 howitzers. Artillery batteries had four pieces. In May 1944, the 3rd Battalion of 3rd MarDiv's 12th Marines was redesignated Pack Howitzer Battalion, 4th Marines. The 5th Battalion was redesignated as the new 3rd Battalion.

(See Campaign Series 134 *Saipan & Tinian 1944*, page 35–36, for details of changes to the organization of the Marine infantry regiments.)

The separate 4th and 22nd Marines possessed organic units that would normally be attached from divisional units if the regiment was assigned to a division. These included engineer, medical, motor transport, pioneer, and tank companies; reconnaissance, ordnance, and supply and service platoons; plus a 75mm pack howitzer battalion. These regimental

US Armor on Guam

	ARMY	MARINE
75mm M4A2 medium tank	53	76
37mm M5A1 light tank	18	0
75mm M3A1 self-propelled gun (halftrack)	0	12
75mm M7 self-propelled howitzer	24	0
105mm M8 self-propelled howitzer	4	0
3-in. M10 tank destroyer	27	0
37mm LVT(A)1 amphibian tank	0	75
LVT(2)/(4) amphibian tractor	0	373
M3/M5A1 personnel carrier (halftrack)	20	0

units were designated, for example, Tank Company, 4th Marines or Pack Howitzer Battalion, 22nd Marines.

The 3rd and 4th Amphibian Tractor Battalions had three companies with nine amtracs in each of their three platoons and three in the HQ. The battalions had a mix of LVT(2)s and new LVT(4)s. A company from the 10th or 11th Amphibian Tractor Battalions augmented both. The 1st Armored Amphibian Tractor Battalion had four companies with six 37mm gun-armed LVT(A)1 amphibian tanks in each of their three platoons.

US Army

The **77th Infantry Division** was an Army Reserve unit largely from New York and New Jersey. It was activated on 25 March 1942 at Fort Jackson, South Carolina. After conducting major maneuvers throughout the South it undertook desert and amphibious training. It was shipped to Hawaii in March 1944 where it received jungle and additional amphibious training. The "Statue of Liberty Division" was initially assigned as the Joint Expeditionary Force General Reserve and remained on Hawaii through the initial phase of the Marianas campaign. Guam would be its first combat operation and it would land with 17,958 men, including those initially attached to the 1st Prov MarBde. The organization of Army infantry regiments and division artillery are detailed on page 37–38 of Campaign Series 134 *Saipan & Tinian 1944*. The attached 706th Tank Battalion had M4A2 Sherman tanks with 17 tanks each in its Companies A–C with three platoons of five and two in the headquarters. Company D had 18 M5A1 light tanks. For the Guam operation, Marine and Army regiments were task organized into regimental combat teams (RCT)[6], referred to simply as combat teams (CT) by 3rd MarDiv. The exact organization of the RCTs did vary, even within the same division, as their structure was determined by their specific mission.

JAPANESE FORCES – SOUTHERN MARIANAS ARMY GROUP

Established in March 1944, **31st Army** controlled IJA units in the Mandate and roughly equated with a US Army Corps. In theory 31st Army controlled five divisions, six IMBs, and five independent infantry regiments, but in reality had little tactical control over its widespread forces. Caught returning from an inspection of the Palaus at the time of the attack, 31st Army commander diverted to Guam where he established

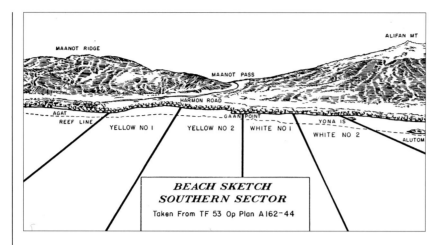

BEACH SKETCH
SOUTHERN SECTOR
Taken From TF 53 Op Plan A162-44

a new headquarters, although his main headquarters was still on Saipan under the chief of staff.

With the increased attacks on the Marianas in September 1943, the Japanese planned to ship the 13th Division from China to defend Guam. Its 300-man advance detachment arrived in October, but the rest of the Division remained in China to support a new offensive.

The **29th Division** had been activated at Nagoya, Honshu, Japan in August 1941 and sent to Manchuria in 1942. It was designated to defend Guam and reorganized as a sea operations division in February 1944. It departed from Korea and made it most of the way before American submarines attacked and a transport went down with 1,800 men of the 18th Infantry and all their equipment. The survivors disembarked on Saipan. The 50th Infantry was delivered to Tinian and the Division and its 38th Infantry arrived on Guam on 4 March. There it was designated as Southern Marianas Army Group. IJN forces on the islands were placed under its control. The partly rebuilt 18th Infantry (less I Battalion) arrived from Saipan in early June.

To augment the 29th Division, the 6th Expeditionary Force was formed in Manchuria from elements of the 1st and 11th Divisions. It arrived on 20 March and was soon reorganized into two new units. The artillery and three infantry battalions from the 11th Division and its 11th Infantry Group Headquarters were reorganized into the 48th IMB and a fourth independent infantry battalion was formed from the fourth rifle company of the three original battalions. The same mix of units from the 1st Division was organized into the 10th IMR. Its I Battalion was sent to garrison Rota on 23 June. US intelligence initially estimated 12,744 IJA troops on Guam. Actual strength was 11,464.

The 29th Division was a sea operations division, with artillery and engineer units organic to the regiments and an almost regiment-sized sea transport unit provided with 120 organic landing barges. The regiments were of two different structures. The 18th Infantry was a heavy strike force, and the 38th Infantry a light unit. Since it had lost many men and most of its equipment, the 18th Infantry's battalions were now organized with a small headquarters, three rifle companies, and a mortar company with nine potent 90mm Type 94 (1939) mortars. The 38th had three battalions each with three rifle companies, a machine-gun company (six 7.7mm HMGs), and an infantry gun company. It also had a battalion-sized artillery unit with at least nine 75mm Type 94 (1934) mountain guns, which were attached to the infantry battalions, plus company-size engineer, signal, transport, medical, and intendance (administrative) units.

The 48th IMB had four independent infantry battalions (IIB) plus engineer, signal, and medical companies. The battalions had three rifle companies and machine-gun and infantry gun companies. The battalion-size brigade artillery unit had nine 75mm mountain guns. The 10th IMR had three battalions organized as those in the 48th IMB and had arrived with only three rifle companies. It also had engineer and signal companies plus a regimental artillery unit with 12 75mm Type 41 (1908) regimental guns.

The three Japanese tank companies were equipped with varied numbers of Type 97 (1937) 57mm gun-armed medium tanks and Type 95 (1935) 37mm gun-armed light tanks. The 29th Division's 24th Tank Company had nine light tanks; another eight had been lost with the sinking of the 18th Infantry's transport. The 1st Company, 9th Tank Regiment, attached to the 38th IMR, had 12–15 light tanks while the 2nd Company, attached to the 48th IMB, possessed 10 or 11 mediums and two or three lights. A Japanese report listed a total of 38 tanks, but not by type.

Imperial Japanese Navy Forces, Guam

IJN forces were under the command of the **54th Guard Force** with 21 coast defense gun companies of from two to four guns apiece (19 x 200mm, 8 x 150mm, 22 x 127mm, 6 x 80mm). Only 150 guard force sailors initially occupied Guam, but this had grown to 450 in February 1944. From then the naval forces began to buildup along with the airfields and the subsequent arrival of large number of service and construction personnel. The 54th Guard Force grew to 2,300 men in March and April when most of the coast defense guns were emplaced. Other IJN units included the 60th Antiaircraft Unit with 12 25mm Type 96 (1936) twin or triple AA guns, 217th and 218th Construction Battalions, and 263rd, 521st, and 755th Air Groups. The air group ground personnel would be organized into named battalion-size rifle units. These units' leaders and troops had no tactical training and were armed with only rifles, a few light machine-guns, and aircraft machine-guns modified for ground firing. Some 7,000 IJN personnel were on Guam, of whom about 2,000 were air service.

---

6 Augmented by tank, combat engineer, and medical companies plus service elements.

7 The number of Japanese heavy weapons on Guam is unclear. Column A is from a captured Japanese list, which may not be accurate. Column B is the pre-landing IIIAC C-2 estimate.

8 This is believed to be a Maxim rapid-fire infantry gun captured from Russia in 1904–05 and worthless as an AT weapon.

THE GUAM ASSAULT

Preliminaries

From 11–13 June 1944 the preparatory naval and air bombardment of Saipan, Tinian, and Guam commenced, as did air attacks on Rota and Pagan. On 12 June 216 carrier aircraft attacked southern Marianas airfields. The same day B-24 bomber raids began battering Saipan and Tinian. Most sources state 150 Japanese aircraft were destroyed on the ground and in the air, but it appears only 36 were destroyed. On the 12th and 13th carrier aircraft interdicted several Japanese convoys fleeing the Marianas, sinking 12 cargo ships plus a few small escort vessels and large numbers of fishing boats, which might be used to transfer troops between islands. On 27 June battleships and cruisers began shelling Guam and air attacks increased. On 4 July the air attacks were further increased with a carrier group dedicated to the mission. It conducted daylight attacks while destroyers shelled targets at night. Two additional carrier groups arrived on the 6 July and began night raids as well. As W-Day grew closer the bombardment increased with more carriers and gun-armed ships arriving. Guam was lashed with the heaviest pre-landing bombard of the Pacific War so far. During this entire period up to W-Day, only 16 US aircraft were lost over Guam. Orote Peninsula received special attention through all this. Most fixed coast defense guns were knocked out well before the landing force arrived.

The view from a Japanese cave position on Chonito Cliff overlooks the 3rd Marines' "Red" Beaches. Adelup Point, taken by 3/3 Marines, is seen in the upper center of the photo. For scale, a 1/4-ton jeep is seen in the lower center.

4th Marines troops wade ashore on to "White 1". They are probably the 3rd Battalion, the Regimental Reserve, since they are debarking from landing craft, personnel or vehicle (LCVP) rather than rolling ashore aboard amtracs.

Underwater Demolition Teams (UDT) 3, 4, and 6 arrived and for three nights beginning on 14 July UDT-3 reconnoitered the landing beaches. From 17 July all three teams, covered by LCI(G) gunboats, demolished 640 obstacles off the Northern Beaches and 300 off the Southern. Little barbed wire and no mines were found. They also conducted a diversionary reconnaissance of Tumon Bay, charted gaps in the reef, blasted boat lanes and marked them with buoys. Only two frogmen were lost.

The Southern Attack Force bearing the STLF assault troops departed Eniwetok for Guam between 11 and 18 July and 274 vessels arrived at Guam on the 20th and 21st. In a change from earlier landings, there was no demonstration to mislead the Japanese as to the location of the actual landings. Such feints had little effect in the past and it was hoped that the two landing beaches an unprecedented 7 miles apart would cause enough uncertainty.

W-DAY

At 05.30hrs 21 July, the gunfire support ships accompanying the Southern Attack Force moved into position and opened fire. The troop ships were assembled in the transport area by 06.00hrs. The day was clear, the sea calm, and the surf light. The landing areas were soon shrouded in smoke and dust from the preparatory bombardment. H-Hour was set for 08.30.

The assault waves crossed the lines of departure at 07.40. LCI(G)s advanced ahead of the waves of amtracs, firing 4.5in. rocket barrages. At 08.22hrs a massive naval bombardment smothered the beaches and their adjacent areas lasting until the first assault waves were 1,200yds (1,097m) from shore. The larger caliber guns (6in. and greater) shifted their fire inland while the 5in. guns continued to shell the beaches until the lead amphibian tanks crossed the reef. Final runs were made by 84 fighter-bombers and 16 torpedo-bombers then they too shifted to targets inland. The LCI(G)s moved to the flanks of the beaches and continued to fire into adjacent areas to pin down the defenders.

The 3rd MarDiv's lead amphibian tanks came ashore on the Northern Beaches at 08.29hrs. The Division's four beaches were situated between Adelup and Asan Points, described as the "devil's horns." 3/3 and 2/3 (3rd CT Reserve) landed on Beach "Red 1" while 1/3 landed on "Red 2". The 21st CT landed on "Green" in a column of battalions (3rd, 2nd, 1st) and the 9th CT came ashore on "Blue" in the same order as the 21st. Units landing on "Green" and "Blue" had to cross broad rice paddies overlooked by Japanese-infested ridges. It was planned for the 3rd Marines' three battalion 81mm mortar platoons to be combined upon landing into a provisional Mortar Groupment on the boundary between "Red 1" and "2" to concentrate fire on Adelup Point. This proved unnecessary because of lighter than expected resistance there. The assistant division commander was ashore by late morning and the division commander assumed control of operations ashore at 17.15hrs.

The 1st Prov MarBde landed on the Southern Beaches at 08.32hrs. 1/22 landed on Beach "Yellow 1" adjacent to Agat Town and 2/22 on "Yellow 2". The reserve 3/22 came ashore on "Yellow 1". 2/4 landed on "White 1" north of Bangi Point and 1/4 on "White 2" followed by the reserve 3/4.

On the Northern Beaches the 3rd Marines' north flank was able to push inland only 200–300yds (183–274m) and were held up by defenses on Chonito Cliff and Bundschu Ridge on the north flank. The 21st Marines in the center cleared Asan Town and gained a foothold on the face of the Fonte Plateau 1,600yds (1,463m) inland. A 200yd (183m) wide gap existed between the two regiments in the gorge of the north fork of the Asan River. The maze of ravines, and coral outcroppings, and tangled vegetation was more of an obstacle to closing the gap than enemy resistance. The two regiments made major efforts to link up over the next bitter days, but this was not accomplished until after the Japanese counterattack of 25/26 June. On the south flank the 9th Marines pushed almost the same distance inland and down the coast toward Apra Harbor. W-Day nightfall found the battalions positioned, left to right: 3/3, 2/3, 1/3, 2/21, 3/21, 1/9, and

2/9. Only 1/21 and 3/9 were held in Division Reserve. The beachhead was about 1,600 by 4,000 yards (1,463 x 3,658m). The Division had lost 105 killed in action (KIA), 56 missing in action (MIA), and 536 wounded in action (WIA). This equated to the loss of almost a battalion, but aggressive leadership pushing the troops forward was credited with reducing casualties: by the time the Japanese called in mortar and artillery fire the targeted Marines had often already rushed forward. Nine LVTs were lost during the landing and more were lost ashore on the first day. The Japanese had abandoned the beach positions, apparently because of the intense bombardment, but as troops fought their way up the stepped ridges one officer reported, "...every ridge gained by the 21st Marines disclosed another pocket of enemy behind it." The principal Japanese units defending the area were the 320th IIB and I/18 Infantry. However, LtGen Takeshi was assembling much of the 48th IMB and other units to "drive the Americans from Fonte."

The 1st Prov MarBde on the Southern Beaches established a deeper overall lodgment, up to 1,500-2,000yds (1,372–1,829m) inland along most its length, but it was only able to extend the flanks of its beachhead a few hundred yards in either direction. It did secure Agat Town on the north flank and Bangi Point on the south. The troops were subject to extremely heavy fire on the beaches, but it slackened once they pushed inland 200–300yds (183–274m). Japanese defensive positions scattered across the area made progress slow. Unlike on the Northern Beaches the Japanese did not abandon their beach positions, but remained in their holes, despite being battered and shocked. These defenses included concrete pillboxes, trenches, and antitank ditches. The 1st Provisional Marine Brigade CP was established ashore at 13.50hrs. The firing was so intense the frontline troops began to run low on ammunition and no resupply had yet been landed. The 22nd Marines on the north flank had responsibility for only a third of the beachhead perimeter as they were

A landing vehicle, tracked Mk II (LVT(2)), or Alligator, is refueled from a pontoon barge moored at the reef line. These barges were fitted with a crane to assist with the transfer of supplies from landing craft, which could not cross the reef's lip, and provided with fuel, rations, and minor amtrac spare parts.

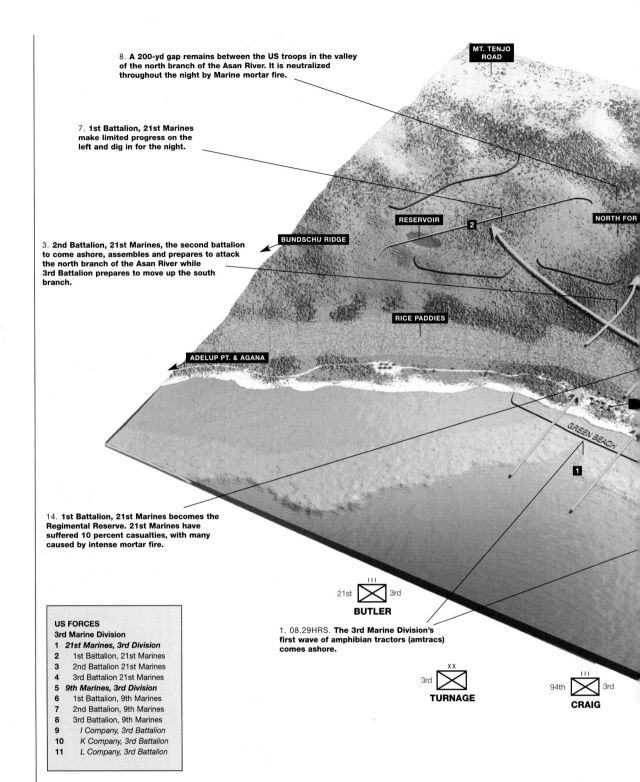

8. **A 200-yd gap remains between the US troops in the valley of the north branch of the Asan River. It is neutralized throughout the night by Marine mortar fire.**

7. **1st Battalion, 21st Marines make limited progress on the left and dig in for the night.**

3. **2nd Battalion, 21st Marines, the second battalion to come ashore, assembles and prepares to attack the north branch of the Asan River while 3rd Battalion prepares to move up the south branch.**

MT. TENJO ROAD

RESERVOIR

2

NORTH FOR

BUNDSCHU RIDGE

RICE PADDIES

ADELUP PT. & AGANA

GREEN BEACH

1

14. **1st Battalion, 21st Marines becomes the Regimental Reserve. 21st Marines have suffered 10 percent casualties, with many caused by intense mortar fire.**

21st |×| 3rd
BUTLER

1. **08.29HRS. The 3rd Marine Division's first wave of amphibian tractors (amtracs) comes ashore.**

US FORCES
3rd Marine Division
1   *21st Marines, 3rd Division*
2   1st Battalion, 21st Marines
3   2nd Battalion 21st Marines
4   3rd Battalion 21st Marines
5   *9th Marines, 3rd Division*
6   1st Battalion, 9th Marines
7   2nd Battalion, 9th Marines
8   3rd Battalion, 9th Marines
9   *I Company, 3rd Battalion*
10   *K Company, 3rd Battalion*
11   *L Company, 3rd Battalion*

3rd |××|
TURNAGE

94th |×| 3rd
CRAIG

SECURING THE BEACHHEAD, 21ST AND 9TH MARINES

21 July 1944, viewed from the southwest showing the 21st and 9th Marines' movements on W-Day to secure the high ground overlooking Beaches 'Green' and 'Blue'.

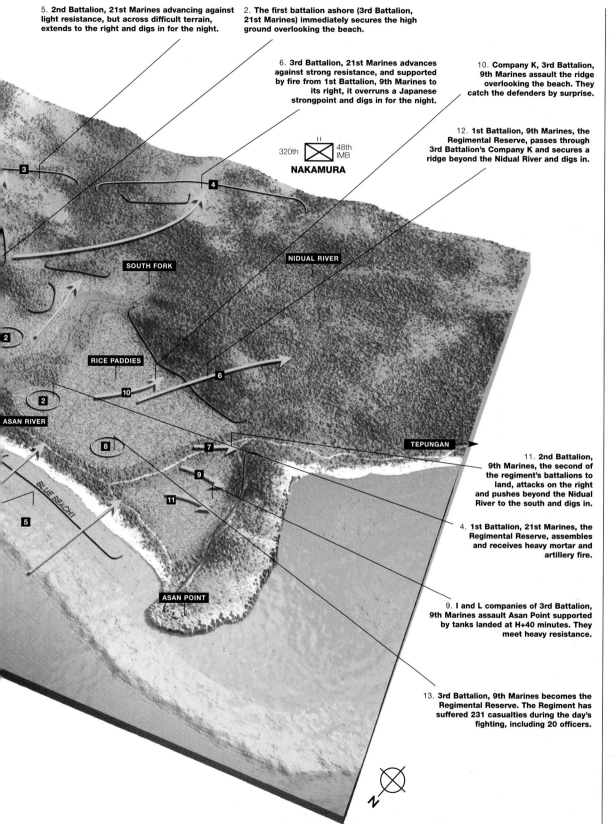

5. 2nd Battalion, 21st Marines advancing against light resistance, but across difficult terrain, extends to the right and digs in for the night.

2. The first battalion ashore (3rd Battalion, 21st Marines) immediately secures the high ground overlooking the beach.

6. 3rd Battalion, 21st Marines advances against strong resistance, and supported by fire from 1st Battalion, 9th Marines to its right, it overruns a Japanese strongpoint and digs in for the night.

10. Company K, 3rd Battalion, 9th Marines assault the ridge overlooking the beach. They catch the defenders by surprise.

12. 1st Battalion, 9th Marines, the Regimental Reserve, passes through 3rd Battalion's Company K and secures a ridge beyond the Nidual River and digs in.

320th ⊠ 48th IMB

NAKAMURA

3

4

SOUTH FORK

NIDUAL RIVER

2

RICE PADDIES

6

2

10

ASAN RIVER

8

7

TEPUNGAN

9

11

11. 2nd Battalion, 9th Marines, the second of the regiment's battalions to land, attacks on the right and pushes beyond the Nidual River to the south and digs in.

BLUE BEACH

5

4. 1st Battalion, 21st Marines, the Regimental Reserve, assembles and receives heavy mortar and artillery fire.

ASAN POINT

9. I and L companies of 3rd Battalion, 9th Marines assault Asan Point supported by tanks landed at H+40 minutes. They meet heavy resistance.

13. 3rd Battalion, 9th Marines becomes the Regimental Reserve. The Regiment has suffered 231 casualties during the day's fighting, including 20 officers.

N

concentrating for the push to Orote Peninsula. The 4th Marines' wide frontage, and the very heavy resistance faced on the forward slopes of Mt. Alifan, led to most reserves being placed in the line. 4th Marines had planned for LVTs to carry the troops 1,000yds (914m) inland, but this was abandoned because of rough terrain and the heavy fire the amtracs drew. Harmon Road, just south of the two regiments' common boundary was secured, however, which was important as it provided a route by which to outflank Mt. Alifan to the north and was expected to serve as a route for a Japanese counterattack. The Brigade Artillery Group came ashore and the Army's 305th Field Artillery Battalion would be attached when landed. The end of the day found the Brigade's battalions deployed from left to right: 1/22, 2/22, 1/4(-), 2/4, and 3/4. The 4th Marines' only reserve was C/1/4. The 22nd Marines was able to keep its 3rd Battalion in reserve. 2/305 Infantry landed on "White 1" late in the day as the Brigade Reserve. Although the plan was to have the entire regiment ashore on W-Day, communications problems and shortages of landing craft and LVTs delayed the landing of the rest of the 305th until the early hours of W+1. There were also difficulties getting the Corps Artillery ashore. Instead of landing the entire 1st 155mm Howitzer Battalion on W-Day, only three howitzers were landed by nightfall. The Brigade had suffered an estimated 350 casualties and 24 LVTs were lost on W-Day – 10 during the landing. Its beachhead was 2,000 by 4,500yds (1,829 x 4,115m). Some companies had fewer than 100 effectives, and the commander of C/1/22 reported only 100 effectives out of the 240 men he landed with in the morning, advising, "Need help for tonight." The principal Japanese units engaged up to this point were I and II/38 Infantry; III/38 would join in the night's counterattacks. Rear Admiral Richard R. Conolly, Southern Attack Force commander, reported, "The ship to shore movement was executed with perfect precision and exactly on schedule." His goal was, "to get the troops ashore standing up."

On W-Day LtGen Takeshi immediately began assembling reserve units on Fonte Plateau once the 3rd MarDiv was ashore. Much of the 320th IIB

Covered by a destroyer, LCVPs bearing the 2/305 Infantry await orders to head to shore. They were afloat 3½ hours before the beaches were clear enough for them to land.

had been lost defending Chonito Cliff against the 3rd Marines. The 319th IIB, the 48th IMB Reserve, had been committed to defend the plateau's forward slope, 2/18 Infantry had been thrown into the center, 9/III/38 reinforced Bundschu Ridge. II and III/10 IMR began moving in daylight from Ordot and 321 and 322 IIBs headed south. The former left a company defending Agaña Bay and IJN rifle units were held in reserve at Tiyan Airfield as Takeshi still feared an American landing in the bay. The 322 IIB had been defending Tumon Bay. Discovered by US aerial observers, the units made slow progress to Fonte Plateau enduring air and naval bombardment to arrive through the night. II and III/18 Infantry, II and III/10 IMR would participate in the night's counter-attacks, but the 321 and 322 IIBs would not arrive in time.

The Japanese launched small counterattacks through the night. On the Northern Beaches the 3rd MarDiv experienced less severe counter-attacks than the Brigade in the south. Harassing artillery and mortar fire continued through the night forcing a halt to unloading at 02.30. Several small counterattacks were easily beaten off. The Japanese lost hundreds of men in these piecemeal attacks and during the movement of the reserves to the plateau. On the Southern Beaches 3/4 was hit with repeated attacks through the night. Hill 40, anchoring the southern flank near the beach, was lost twice, but recaptured and held. A Japanese infantry attack supported by four tanks drove down Harmon Road and hit 1/4 at 02.30hrs. A bazookaman knocked out two tanks and Shermans destroyed the others forcing the infantry to retreat. It was discovered later that the commander of the 38th Infantry was killed in this attack. Another infantry attack hit 1/4 almost penetrating to the artillery positions 400yds from the beach. Company A, 1/4 killed over 200 Japanese, but it lost an entire platoon and fought the rest of the campaign as a two-platoon company. Numerous platoon and company attacks hit the 22nd Marines on the north flank through the night. In all the Japanese lost at least 400 men that night. LtGen Takeshi initially denied the request to conduct this piecemeal counterattack, but later relented in hopes of delaying the American advance. Despite his request to attack, the regimental commander was apparently not confident of success as he burned the regimental colors before attacking.

EXPANDING THE BEACHHEADS (W+1 TO W+8)

On the northern beachhead the 3rd Marines was having difficulties accomplishing its missions, as its strength was so low with some companies down to 30–40 men. Bundschu Ridge and Chonito Cliff were only about 100ft (31m) high, but here, as well as on the forward slope of Fonte Plateau, the terrain was extremely rugged and covered by dense tangled vegetation. Guadalcanal veterans said it was the worst terrain they had ever experienced. On W+1 1/3 and 2/3 attempted to take Bundschu Ridge with 20mm and 40mm covering fire from the 14th Defense Battalion, but without success. Casualties were so high that the 3rd Marines commander formed a provisional rifle company from the regimental weapons company and attached it to 1/3 in an effort to clear the troublesome ridge. Colonel

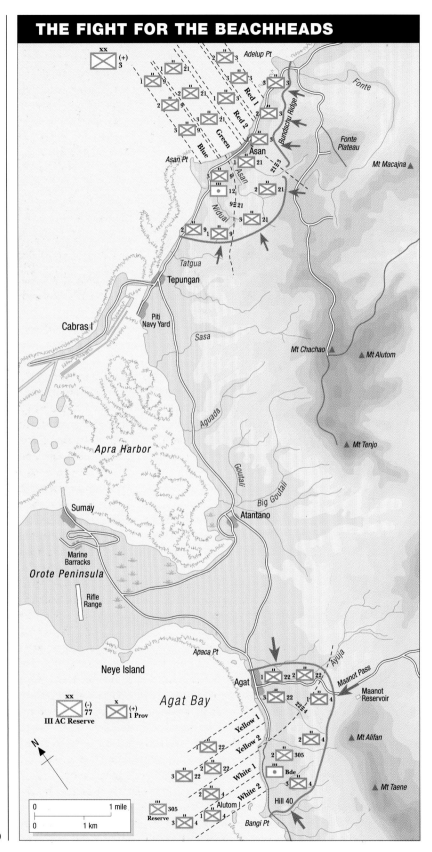

A 77th InfDiv service troops bivouac on the "White" Beaches. Beachheads were typically cluttered and appeared disorganized owing to the rush of activities, limited space, and a constant flow of new units, supplies, and equipment coming ashore.

Hall said, "I am going to try and advance up that mess in front of me. What I really need is a battalion whereas I have only 160 men to use on a 500-yard slope. Company A is down to 30–40 men with the air liaison officer in charge." A/1/3 had been commanded by Capt Geary R. Bundschu and was the unit originally assigned to assault the ridge overlooking Asan Village. They tried again on W+2 and discovered the ridge had been largely abandoned, but after mopping-up were in no state to advance further. The 3rd Marines requested reinforcement from the 307th Infantry still afloat, but MajGen Geiger was reluctant to commit any of the 77th InfDiv in the north when he knew it would be needed in the south. It would take five companies four days of hard fighting to secure the small ridge. The 21st Marines made little progress up the plateau's slopes. 2/21 was 40 per cent depleted and was pulled from the line. On 22 July, the 21st Marines attempted to clear the ravine separating it from the 3rd Marines, but was driven back. Two 3rd Marines companies finally managed to establish contact in the afternoon. On the right the 2/9 Marines secured the Piti Navy Yard with little opposition. At 14.25hrs, 3/9 was landed by LVTs on Cabras Island conducting a shore-to-shore assault. The island was cleared the next day, 23 July; with the exception of numerous snipers and hundreds of mines, it was unoccupied. The island was then turned over to the 14th Defense Battalion from where it provided air defense of the northern beachhead and the harbor and could fire directly on Orote Peninsula. On 24 July a small patrol was sent south accompanied by amphibious tanks to contact the 1st Prov MarBde, but was driven back by enemy fire and hampered by the massed friendly fire being directed at Orote Peninsula.

In the south the 1st Prov MarBde aimed to expand its beachhead in all directions. The 22nd Marines advanced north meeting moderate resistance, but found the bridge over the Ayuja River had been destroyed. Like most rivers on Guam, it was narrow and shallow, but the banks were high and steep. The water here was sufficiently deep to prevent supporting tanks from crossing and they were replaced with amphibian tanks. This was an exception to the rule that amphibian tanks were not to

be employed inland because of their vulnerability. The Shermans were able to cross the next day after a causeway had bridged the river. The 305th Infantry (- 2d Battalion) attacked up Harmon Road toward Maanot Pass. While the attack began late because of the time required for the regiment to reorganize after the night landing, it was successful and passed beyond the objective line in the afternoon. The 4th Marines assaulted Mt. Alifan on W+1. Resistance was moderate, but the terrain extremely rugged, making progress slow. A 1/4 Marine patrol did reach the peak and found it unoccupied. On 23 July the 4th Marines did not advance, but prepared to be relieved by the 306th Infantry. The 306th Infantry's landing on the "White" beaches required the entire day because of communications problems and landing craft shortages. It was not until the next day that 4th Marines was fully replaced by the 306th. IIIAC Artillery was landing over "White 1" at this same time, as was the 77th InfDiv Artillery, leading to a great deal of congestion, especially when coupled with the landing of smaller units, supplies, and ammunition. Most artillery battalions were in-place by nightfall as was the 9th Defense Battalion deployed along the beaches. The defense battalions, besides providing air defense and direct fire support on ground targets, were positioned to engage any Japanese counter-landing attempts on the beachhead. The 77th InfDiv, with the 305th on the right (center of the beachhead) and the 306th on the left, would secure the southern portion allowing the 4th Marines to move north with the 22nd Marines to seal off the neck of Orote Peninsula.

On 24 July 1/22 advanced up the Agat–Sumay Road running along the coast to the peninsula. The terrain consisted of rice paddies interspaced with small hillocks and defended by II/38 Infantry. Intense naval, artillery, and aerial bombardment pounded the area before the advance began. The Japanese made good use of their short-ranged weapons and US tanks could provide little support because of the muddy flooded rice paddies. 3/22 swung to the right and moved toward the

Troops of the 4th Marines move toward the line of hills behind the Southern Beaches, north to south: Mounts Alifan, Taene, Almagosa and Lamlam. The 869ft (265m) Mt. Alifan can be seen in the background as a SBD Dauntless scout-bomber buzzes past.

Twin 20mm Mk 4 AA guns of Battery I, 14th Defense Battalion were emplaced atop Chonito Ridge once it was captured. From there they supported the advance of the 3rd Marines north. Adelup Point is in the upper center. These guns were unique to the Marine Corps. They were the same type mounted aboard ships, but were fitted on the wheeled mounts of the obsolete 37mm M1 AA gun.

Apra Harbor side of the peninsula's neck. The Japanese defenders counterattacked 2/22 immediately their attack was launched at 10.00hrs. 2/22 quickly reorganized and secured some high ground at the southeast end of the harbor blocking the road leading north out of the peninsula. 1/22 and 3/22 closed off most of the peninsula's neck as planned, although a gap remained between 3/22 and the harbor, but this was covered with heavy firepower and the Japanese did not attempt to escape through it.

The 307th Infantry landed on 24 July, occupying an assembly area on the north side on Harmon Road just east of Agat, and the Division CP was established ashore that afternoon. MajGen Bruce requested two of the 307th's battalions to expand the FBL further east as enemy resistance was virtually nil in that zone. Geiger was reluctant to give up his only corps reserve with the fight for Orote Peninsula just beginning. However, in the light of the delays encountered bringing other regiments ashore, he did agree that it should be landed to be in-place when needed. The 305th RCT was released from the 1st Prov MarBde and returned to the 77th InfDiv's control.

The 3rd Marines fighting on the Fonte Plateau on 25 July were encountering moderate resistance, but were still hampered by the rough terrain. The main resistance facing the 21st Marines was the Mt. Chachao-Alutom-Tenjo complex. Headway was made, but it was a slow grueling process. The 9th Marines easily advanced south halfway along the shore of Apra Harbor to the Aguada River. This overextended its lines, however, and it was ordered to pull back 1,500yds (1,372m) to the Laguas River.

Also on 25 July, the neck of Orote Peninsula was completely closed off in preparation for the peninsula's capture. A large inland mangrove swamp hindered this operation. 3/22 ran into a dense cluster of pillboxes and the depleted 1/22 was relieved by 1/4. Up to 12 Japanese tanks were destroyed in the fighting. A 9th Marines patrol moving down from the north made contact with 22nd Marines, but this did not constitute a secure link-up between the two landing forces.

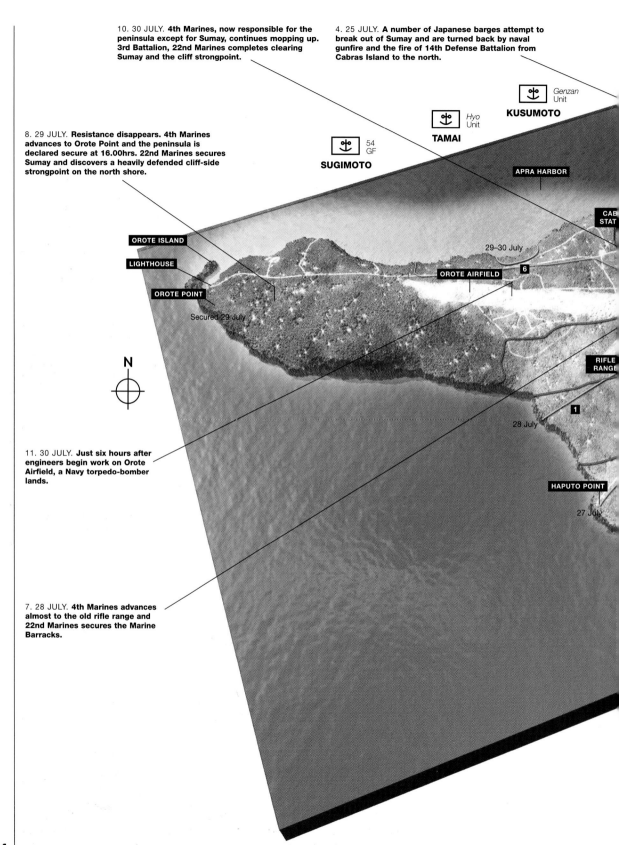

10. 30 JULY. 4th Marines, now responsible for the peninsula except for Sumay, continues mopping up. 3rd Battalion, 22nd Marines completes clearing Sumay and the cliff strongpoint.

4. 25 JULY. A number of Japanese barges attempt to break out of Sumay and are turned back by naval gunfire and the fire of 14th Defense Battalion from Cabras Island to the north.

Genzan
Unit

KUSUMOTO

Hyo
Unit

TAMAI

8. 29 JULY. Resistance disappears. 4th Marines advances to Orote Point and the peninsula is declared secure at 16.00hrs. 22nd Marines secures Sumay and discovers a heavily defended cliff-side strongpoint on the north shore.

54
GF

SUGIMOTO

APRA HARBOR

CAB
STAT

 OROTE ISLAND

LIGHTHOUSE

OROTE POINT

Secured 29 July

29–30 July

OROTE AIRFIELD

6

RIFLE
RANGE

1

N

28 July

11. 30 JULY. Just six hours after engineers begin work on Orote Airfield, a Navy torpedo-bomber lands.

HAPUTO POINT

27 July

7. 28 JULY. 4th Marines advances almost to the old rifle range and 22nd Marines secures the Marine Barracks.

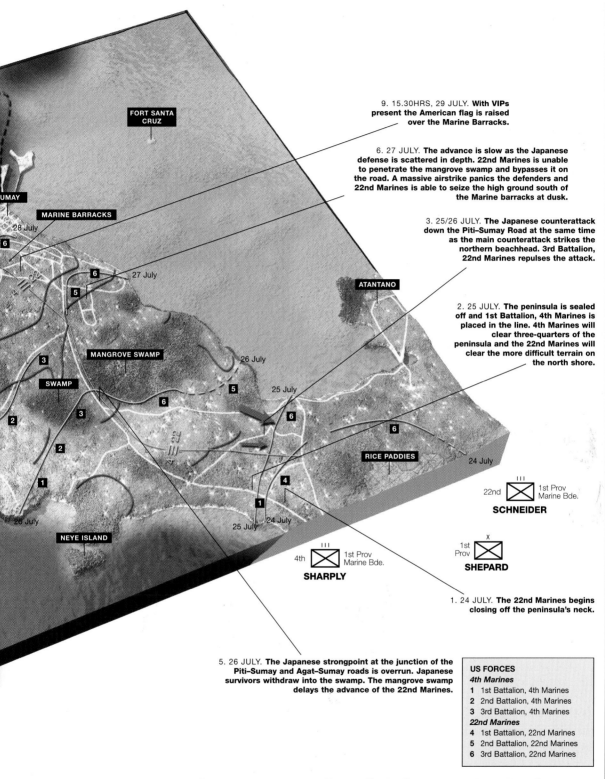

FORT SANTA CRUZ

9. 15.30HRS, 29 JULY. **With VIPs present the American flag is raised over the Marine Barracks.**

6. 27 JULY. **The advance is slow as the Japanese defense is scattered in depth. 22nd Marines is unable to penetrate the mangrove swamp and bypasses it on the road. A massive airstrike panics the defenders and 22nd Marines is able to seize the high ground south of the Marine barracks at dusk.**

3. 25/26 JULY. **The Japanese counterattack down the Piti–Sumay Road at the same time as the main counterattack strikes the northern beachhead. 3rd Battalion, 22nd Marines repulses the attack.**

2. 25 JULY. **The peninsula is sealed off and 1st Battalion, 4th Marines is placed in the line. 4th Marines will clear three-quarters of the peninsula and the 22nd Marines will clear the more difficult terrain on the north shore.**

UMAY

MARINE BARRACKS

28 July

6

6 27 July

5

ATANTANO

3

MANGROVE SWAMP

26 July

SWAMP

5

25 July

3

6

2

6

2

6

1

RICE PADDIES

24 July

1

4

26 July

25 July   24 July

NEYE ISLAND

```
        III
22nd   [X]   1st Prov
             Marine Bde.
      SCHNEIDER
```

```
              X
1st    [X]
Prov
      SHEPARD
```

```
        III
4th    [X]   1st Prov
             Marine Bde.
      SHARPLY
```

1. 24 JULY. **The 22nd Marines begins closing off the peninsula's neck.**

5. 26 JULY. **The Japanese strongpoint at the junction of the Piti–Sumay and Agat–Sumay roads is overrun. Japanese survivors withdraw into the swamp. The mangrove swamp delays the advance of the 22nd Marines.**

US FORCES
4th Marines
1 1st Battalion, 4th Marines
2 2nd Battalion, 4th Marines
3 3rd Battalion, 4th Marines
22nd Marines
4 1st Battalion, 22nd Marines
5 2nd Battalion, 22nd Marines
6 3rd Battalion, 22nd Marines

THE CAPTURE OF OROTE PENINSULA

24–30 July, viewed from the south showing 22nd and 4th Marines progress in capturing this vital Japanese stronghold, which separated the northern and southern beachheads.

Four "Long Tom" 155mm M1A1 guns of Battery A, 7th 155mm Gun Battalion are moved into position inland from Beach "White 2". All three IIIAC Artillery battalions (two 155mm howitzer, one 155mm gun) were landed on the Southern Beaches enabling them to support not only the 1st Prov MarBde there, but the 3rd MarDiv to the north. In this way they would be not be hampered by the expected heavy counterattacks and counterbattery fire the Northern Beaches would receive. In the background is the Mount Alifan-Taene-Almagosa-Lamlam ridge.

The night of 25 July found 3rd MarDiv deployed on a 9,000yd (8,230m) frontline with few reserves, a situation made all the more difficult because of the chaotic terrain. Only 1/3 was in Division Reserve along with tank, engineer, and pioneer units. One reason the resistance had been so strong during the day is that the Japanese were fighting hard to retain positions from which to launch their planned counterattack. However, the Japanese lost many first rate troops in the defense of these positions who would have participated in the planned counterattack. LtGen Takeshi developed a plan and assembled units to conduct a major counterattack on the night of 25/26 July, with the goal of splitting 3rd MarDiv positions and attacking the divided forces. The 48th IMB would hit 2/9 and 2/21 with its 219th and 220th IIBs and swing northeast to attack the rear of the 3rd Marines, specifically targeting ammunition and supply dumps. The 18th Infantry would attack the center of the 21st Marines and drive to the coast among the headquarters, artillery, and service units. The main attacks were launched from the vicinity of an unnamed hill where the Mt. Tenjo Road crested the Fonte Plateau, a feature known to the Japanese as "Mt. Mangan." Hundreds of attackers carried demolition charges and hand mines so that, after destroying their targets, the 18th Infantry could establish a defense line. This would run from Asan Point east along a ridge south of the Nidual River, facing south to block 9th Marines counterattacks. A company of the 10th IMR would attack down the 600yd (549m) wide draw separating the 21st and 9th Marines that was screened by only the 3rd Reconnaissance Company (-). Other 10th IMR battalions apparently followed the 18th Infantry battalions, moving through the gaps they created. The 2,500-man Orote Peninsula force would attack the 22nd Marines blocking the peninsula's neck and attempt a breakout to join forces with those on Fonte Plateau, both across country and by barge across Agat Harbor.

The counterattack was coordinated much better than the disorganized *banzai* changes the Marines had encountered in the past. Regardless, many of the Japanese troops were drunk and some units launched their attacks late. As night fell the intensity of the fighting did not diminish. A company commander in 1/9 reported, "The enemy was within hand grenade range along the entire line to the front and retained strong positions in caves to our rear." The fighting went on all night beginning just before midnight, though constant probes and harassing attacks preceded this. Japanese units penetrated almost to the beach in the center. Service troops participated in the Marine counterattacks while howitzers were wheeled up and fired pointblank into the attackers. Some 50–70 Japanese overran the 3rd MarDiv field hospital with wounded patients fleeing to the beaches dragging the seriously wounded. The lightly wounded armed themselves and fought back. The presence of Marine tanks throughout the area was instrumental in defeating the attack with machine-gun and main gun fire. 1/9 and 24th Tank Companies attempted to advance from Ordot to lend their weight, but they became lost in the dark and returned to their start point. On Orote Peninsula some 500 Japanese of II/38 Infantry attacked near the left flank of the 22nd Marines. Drunk on *sake,* they launched a screaming *banzai* charge out of a mangrove swamp into L/3/22 Marines. Flanking fire was delivered by a platoon of A/1/4 Marines from the south along with massed artillery fire and by 02.00hrs the attackers were virtually destroyed. In the 4th Marines' platoon sector alone were 256 dead Japanese, and the Marine platoon had not lost a single man. The II/38 Infantry was destroyed as an effective fighting force and only scattered remnants of the battalion left to defend the peninsula along with poorly trained and inadequately armed IJN troops. The fighting in the 3rd MarDiv sector did not let up until noon on 26 July. (See the Bird's Eye View on pages 62–63). Daylight allowed the Marines to mop-up remaining stragglers and infiltrators throughout the beachhead. In the 3/21 Marine's sector, however, a significant enemy force had occupied Hill 460 on the boundary between the 3rd and 9th Marines. The Japanese on this hill were

A ridge side of the Fonte Plateau over which the Japanese counterattack had burst. Japanese bodies litter the slopes, which have clearly been blasted by direct artillery fire.

BANZAI ATTACK ON THE 3RD MARINE DIVISION HOSPITAL, 26 JULY (pages 58–59)

As the Japanese III/18th Infantry rushed through the gap between the 21st and 9th Marines, they headed for the beach area to destroy artillery positions and dumps. Japanese were spotted on the high ground south of the 3rd MarDiv's field hospital just before dawn on 26 July. Two companies of pioneers, under the command of LtCol George O. Van Orden, the division infantry training officer, were sent up from the beach to counter this threat. Patients were turned out of the tents and told to head for the beach with the walking wounded carrying the more serious cases. All medical personnel assigned to the Marines were Navy. Medical corpsmen (1) did not wear red-cross armbands for fear of snipers and most carried .30-cal. M1 carbines (2) to protect their patients. The semi-automatic carbine with a 15-round magazine was a popular weapon, but had its limitations. It had poor stopping power, limited penetration of dense brush and bamboo, and a comparatively short range because of its smaller cartridge compared to that used in rifles and machine guns. It was intended as a self-defense weapon and not a main combat arm. From 1943 no pistols were assigned to infantry and artillery regiments. Carbines were carried by everyone not armed with an M1 rifle or BAR. Pioneers (3) were the core of a Marine division's shore party. Their main job was to unload landing craft and move supplies and ammunition to dumps. They could also blast beach obstacles, bulldoze roads, build landing craft beach ramps, dig-in supply dumps, and other

minor construction tasks. Trained as infantrymen, they were often employed as reserves, defending beaches from counterlandings, mopping-up by-passed enemy, and blocking penetrations of the frontline. The mainstay weapon of infantrymen, and other troops, was the .30cal M1 Garand rifle (4). It was semi-automatic and fed by an eight-round clip, and while comparatively heavy, it was without doubt the best combat rifle used in World War II. While most of the wounded Marines (5) were ordered to the beach, 41 patients took up whatever weapons they could find and rushed into the fight alongside armed medical personnel. The wounded were usually disarmed at forward aid stations, but some reported into the nearest medical facility with their weapon. Fortunately this Marine had retained his .30cal M1918A2 Browning automatic rifle, or BAR (6). While heavy, bulky, and possessing only a 20-round magazine (most period squad automatic weapons had 30-round magazines or were belt-fed), it was ruggedly reliable and highly regarded. In an effort to reduce its 21lb weight it was not uncommon for the bipod to be removed. The ragtag defenders of the hospital held out against a determined Japanese attack and successfully fought it off until the pioneers arrived. Only one wounded patient was killed along with a medical officer and a corpsman. A medical officer, a medical warrant officer, a dental officer, 12 corpsmen, and 16 marines assigned to medical units were wounded in the fight for the hospital. The two pioneer companies pursued the withdrawing Japanese up the Nidual River. (Howard Gerrard)

The morning of 26 July in the 3rd MarDiv Field Hospital area after the failed Japanese counterattack. Scores of Japanese troops swept through the area firing into treatment and ward tents; most of the patients had evacuated to the beaches. Walking wounded, hospital staff, and Seabees beat back the attack suffering only light casualties.

able to fire on Marines in the area as daylight revealed targets to them. They managed to pin down the 3/21 Marines CP located 70yds (64m) to the east. Company L, 1/9 Marines were dispatched to attack the hill from the west. The approach over rough ground was difficult and the Japanese detected the company at 50 yards. The attack was launched just before noon and, when the hill was overrun, more than 20 dead Japanese were counted and the rest were driven into a firing line established by K/3/21 Marines with few escaping. Another concentration of Japanese was discovered in the hospital area and was mopped up mainly by service troops.

The Japanese lost some 3,500 troops along with about 95 per cent of the attacking units' officers to include most company and battalion commanders and the commanders of the 48th IMB, 18th Infantry, and 10th IMR. Three 48th IMB battalions were virtually wiped out; for example 321 IIB could muster only 40 men. Marine casualties are unclear as casualties suffered during the 25–26 July were often reported with those on the 27th. It may have been 200–300 dead and a few hundred wounded. All the Japanese could do now was fight a defensive battle as they were pushed to the north. The breakout attempt by the defenders of Orote Peninsula had failed. Some had attempted to flee in barges at 17.00hrs, before the counterattack, and were driven back. The survivors were trapped on the peninsula and doomed.

At 08.00hrs, 26 June, Gen Obata reported the results of the failed counterattack to Imperial General Headquarters in Tokyo. "On the night of 25 June, the Army, with its entire force, launched the general attack from Fonte and Mt. Mangan toward Adelup Point. Commanding officers and all officers and men boldly charged the enemy. The fighting continued until dawn, but our forces failed to achieve the desired objectives, losing more than 80 percent of the personnel, for which I sincerely apologize. I will defend Mt. Mangan to the last by assembling the remaining strength. I feel deeply sympathetic for the officers and men who fell in action and their bereaved families."

Imperial General Headquarters acknowledged the message and commended the troops for their sacrifice. However, it was urged that the **61**

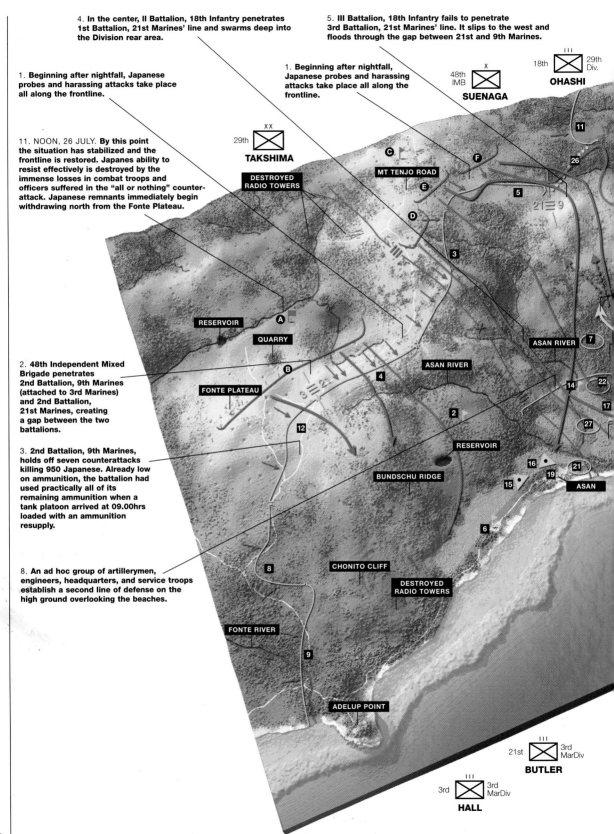

4. In the center, II Battalion, 18th Infantry penetrates 1st Battalion, 21st Marines' line and swarms deep into the Division rear area.

5. III Battalion, 18th Infantry fails to penetrate 3rd Battalion, 21st Marines' line. It slips to the west and floods through the gap between 21st and 9th Marines.

1. Beginning after nightfall, Japanese probes and harassing attacks take place all along the frontline.

1. Beginning after nightfall, Japanese probes and harassing attacks take place all along the frontline.

48th IMB — **SUENAGA**

18th — 29th Div. — **OHASHI**

29th — **TAKSHIMA**

11. NOON, 26 JULY. By this point the situation has stabilized and the frontline is restored. Japanes ability to resist effectively is destroyed by the immense losses in combat troops and officers suffered in the "all or nothing" counter-attack. Japanese remnants immediately begin withdrawing north from the Fonte Plateau.

DESTROYED RADIO TOWERS

MT TENJO ROAD

2. 48th Independent Mixed Brigade penetrates 2nd Battalion, 9th Marines (attached to 3rd Marines) and 2nd Battalion, 21st Marines, creating a gap between the two battalions.

RESERVOIR

QUARRY

FONTE PLATEAU

3. 2nd Battalion, 9th Marines, holds off seven counterattacks killing 950 Japanese. Already low on ammunition, the battalion had used practically all of its remaining ammunition when a tank platoon arrived at 09.00hrs loaded with an ammunition resupply.

ASAN RIVER

ASAN RIVER

RESERVOIR

BUNDSCHU RIDGE

ASAN

8. An ad hoc group of artillerymen, engineers, headquarters, and service troops establish a second line of defense on the high ground overlooking the beaches.

CHONITO CLIFF

DESTROYED RADIO TOWERS

FONTE RIVER

ADELUP POINT

21st — 3rd MarDiv — **BUTLER**

3rd — 3rd MarDiv — **HALL**

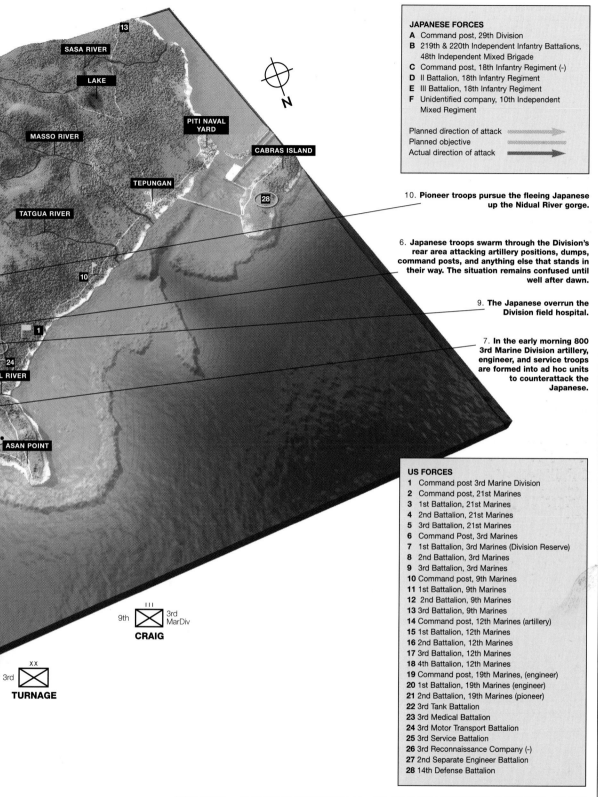

SASA RIVER

LAKE

MASSO RIVER

PITI NAVAL YARD

CABRAS ISLAND

TEPUNGAN

TATGUA RIVER

28

10

1

24

L RIVER

ASAN POINT

N

10. **Pioneer troops pursue the fleeing Japanese up the Nidual River gorge.**

6. **Japanese troops swarm through the Division's rear area attacking artillery positions, dumps, command posts, and anything else that stands in their way. The situation remains confused until well after dawn.**

9. **The Japanese overrun the Division field hospital.**

7. **In the early morning 800 3rd Marine Division artillery, engineer, and service troops are formed into ad hoc units to counterattack the Japanese.**

9th   III   3rd MarDiv

CRAIG

3rd   XX

TURNAGE

THE JAPANESE COUNTERATTACK

Night of 25/26 July, viewed from the north showing the *banzai* attack on 3rd Marine Division.

Troops of the 22nd Marines advance through a coconut palm grove as they approach the old Marine Barracks on Orote Peninsula. While the vegetation was light in some areas, the Japanese used the low brush to their advantage by concealing their fighting positions beneath it and benefited from the open fields of fire.

defense of Guam be prolonged to the extent possible, as "a matter of urgency for the defense of the Home Islands." This directive would cause the Japanese to change their plans.

While mopping-up continued on the morning after the counterattack in the 3rd MarDiv sector, the 1st Prov MarBde was preparing to attack Orote Peninsula. (See the Bird's Eye View on pages 54–55). Preceded by seven Army and Marine artillery battalions firing barrages, supported by 90mm AA guns on Cabras Island, the 4th and 22nd Marines advanced on to the peninsula with the 4th Marines jumping off at 07.00hrs. The 22nd Marines was delayed an hour because of enemy artillery fire. The 4th's right flank became exposed as it advanced and it took over more of the line to the right. Artillery and mortar fire, as well as the mangrove swamp, continued to slow 22nd Marines, but by nightfall the regiment had caught up, although its line bent back east behind the swamp. At 07.15 the attack resumed, but again the swamp delayed the 22nd Marines, which had to move troops on the inland road to bypass it. The higher ground in the vicinity of the old Marine Barracks and rifle range was strongly fortified with trenches and pillboxes holding up both regiments. Late in the day the Japanese began to withdraw, but it was too late to pursue. By the end of 28 July the high ground had been secured just short of the airfield and Army tanks had reinforced the Marine tanks to blast out the many pillboxes. By this time just over half of the peninsula had been cleared and 4th Marines overran the airfield the next day, the regiment pushing on to the peninsula's tip. Orote Peninsula was declared secure at 16.00hrs, 29 July. The 22nd Marines secured Sumay and the north central shore, but the shattered town was so strewn with mines that tanks were forced to remain outside and provide only overhead fire support to the advancing infantrymen. The American flag was hoisted over the ruins of the Marine Barracks at 15.30hrs with "To the Colors" played on a captured Japanese bugle. In a speech to the assembled begrimed troops, Brigadier General Shepard said, "On this hallowed ground, you officers and men of the 1st Marine Brigade have avenged the

OPPOSITE **An M4A2 tank busts through the scrub brush on Orote Peninsula as men of the 4th Marines follow. Most walk in the path flattened by the Sherman, but teams of men maintained security on the flanks.**

loss of our comrades who were overcome by the numerically superior enemy three days after Pearl Harbor."

Over 2,500 Japanese died on Orote. Over 250 pillboxes and fighting positions were found in the 4th Marines' zone alone. The Marines lost 115 KIA, 38 MIA, and 721 WIA. IIIAC Headquarters was established ashore on 26 July.

Back in the north the 3rd MarDiv prepared to push on to the Fonte Plateau in the aftermath of the ill-fated Japanese counterattack. The Japanese began withdrawing north into the island's interior, but rearguards and stragglers offered stiff resistance. The survivors were ordered to fall back to prepared positions near Barrigada and Finegayan "to engage in delaying action in the jungle in northern Guam to hold the island as long as possible." This action was in response to the Imperial General Headquarters directive to prolong the island's defense. Japanese civilians not employed by military units were directed further north. The already weakened 3rd Marines still faced hard going on the ridges and continued to suffer casualties. On the 28 July LtGen Takeshi was killed during the withdrawal from the plateau and LtGen Obata, commander of the 31st Army, was forced to assume command as the only general remaining on the island. By this point the Japanese had lost almost half their trained combat troops, including most of their senior officers, and Obata had only remnants with which to fight a delaying action until the inevitable end.

The American flag is raised at IIIAC Headquarters on Guam on 27 July and US sovereignty over Guam proclaimed.

On 27 July a battalion from each of the 3rd MarDiv's regiments advanced onto the plateau making slow progress. In the 21st Marines' zone, a group of Japanese held out in a quarry for three days before they were blasted out. On 28 July all three regiments continued the attack

TRAIL-BREAKING, NORTHERN GUAM (pages 66–67)

The terrain and dense vegetation of northern Guam, coupled with Japanese tactics, required a less than orthodox employment of tanks. The terrain was rolling and in itself not particularly rugged in many areas. Steep-sided ravines and hillocks making tank movement difficult, if not impossible, cut through other areas. The extremely dense foliage made foot movement by infantrymen carrying combat loads next to impossible. A major problem was land navigation. Down in the brush it was impossible to see more than a few yards ahead and equally impossible to see the few landmark terrain features. Units would drift off course, inadvertently cross unit boundaries, and simply could not determine where they were located in order to accurately report enemy locations and call for supporting fire. They often advanced along the narrow roads and trails until making contact with the dug-in enemy. The Japanese also avoided much of the more difficult terrain for the same reasons. They would establish roadblocks on the roads and trails protected by antitank mines and one or two antitank guns. The range of the defender's machine-guns, rifles, and grenade dischargers was restricted by the limited visibility. The American spearhead would run into such a roadblock, in effect being ambushed, lose a few troops and perhaps one or two tanks, back-off, blast the area with artillery, and send infantry to outflank the position while the force on the trail would suppress the defenders with fire. The Japanese would withdraw back to another prepared position. To

protect the tank under these circumstances the lead rifle company would have a platoon of four or five Sherman M4A2 medium tanks (1) attached to it from the 706th Tank Battalion. A tank advanced through the brush on either side of the trail busting a path for the infantrymen. The platoon's remaining tanks would follow in column 100yds to the rear and periodically relieve the lead tanks. Four infantrymen (2) would be assigned to each lead tank as ground guides, mine spotters, and close-range protection. A field telephone was usually retrofitted to the tank's right rear fender to allow the infantrymen to communicate with the crew (3). White stars on the hull sides were painted over to eliminate an easy aiming point for the enemy (4). The two tanks could also protect each other by placing twice as much fire on the enemy position than a single lead tank. If swarmed by enemy infantry they would machine-gun the attackers off each other; a practice known as "back scratching." This was accomplished by the tanks' bow and coaxial (5) .30-cal. M1919A4 machine guns. The .50-cal. M2 machine normally found atop the turret was removed to prevent enemy infantry for mounting a buttoned-up tank and turning the gun on accompanying infantrymen. The tank's five-man crew was armed with .45-cal. M1911A1 pistols, but they were also provided with a single .45-cal. M1 Thompson or M3 ("grease gun") sub-machine gun plus internal storage for four Mk II fragmentation, four Mk III concussion, four M8 white smoke, and two M14 thermite incendiary hand grenades. (Howard Gerrard)

and at the end of the day the FBL was reached, running from Adelup Point in the north to Magpo Point in the south. Also on 28 July, 21st Marines overran the CP of the 29th Division near the head of the Fonte River. The Marines discovered three large 20-power telescopes on the heights capable of observing not only advancing marines, to the point of distinguishing an individual's features, but the rear areas as well. 3/307 had moved north on 26 July to help close the gap between the 3rd MarDiv and 1st Prov MarBde and on 28 July was attached to 3rd MarDiv. On the 29th the 9th Marines swept back across the ground they had cleared two days before and linked up with 3/307. Most of the rest of the 307th moved north as well and 2/307 secured Mt. Tenjo, while in the south the 306th secured Mounts Alifan and Taene. There was virtually no resistance to the east and south of the beachhead.

THE DRIVE NORTH (W+9 TO W+17)

As the battered Japanese withdrew north, LtGen Obata established his CP at Ordot. He managed to assemble 1,000 infantrymen from different units, 800 IJN rifle troops, and 2,500 service and support troops. Several thousand more scattered Japanese were still at-large on the island and some would join those retreating north. The 48th IMB Artillery Unit had only six pieces left. He still retained two intact tank companies and these would appear at unexpected times and places in small numbers throughout the remainder of the campaign. On 30 July (W+9) the Japanese remnants began an organized withdrawal north across the low ground of the island's isthmus.

A defensive line was to be established anchored on Dededo Village to the east of Tumon Bay and running southeast along the Finegayan–Barrigada Road to Barrigada Village to the southeast of 674ft (206m) Mt. Barrigada. The village of Barrigada is 2,000 yards (1,829m) from the east coast, but this area was left undefended, as the trackless terrain was so rugged and the vegetation extremely dense. With little in the way of regiment, brigade, or even battalion headquarters remaining, Obata organized his troops into the Left and Right Sector Units, defending the areas of Dededo and Finegayan Villages and the slopes of Mt. Barrigada respectively. A second defense line was established on the rising ground just below Ipapao Village. The last stand would be made on 870ft (265m) Mt. Santa Rosa backed against the east coast above Lumuna Point and many of the sick and wounded had been moved to behind Mt. Santa Rosa. On 1 August, with the establishing of the main defense line underway, Obata moved his CP to Mt. Mataguac northeast of Ipapao and west of Mt. Santa Rosa. On the same day he formed the Mt. Santa Rosa Garrison

Some 2,500 Japanese died trapped in the carnage of Orote Peninsula. Their contribution to the defense of Guam was to delay the link-up of the two landing forces and the opening of Apra Harbor for a few days. The cost to the Marines was 153 dead and missing.

Force[9] to prepare the defenses there. They constructed both actual and dummy positions on the two volcanic rock hills.

Obata's strategy was similar to that adopted on Saipan; withdraw into rugged country establishing successive lines of defense, and make the advance as costly for the Americans as possible. Obata's problem was that Guam was wider than Saipan, he had fewer troops, and his predecessor had squandered most of the effective combat troops in the first six days of action. On Saipan the defenders held out for three weeks before launching their own self-destructive counterattack. While there were almost twice as many defenders on Saipan, they did inflict well over twice as many casualties on an American force only marginally larger (28 infantry battalions) than that on Guam (24 battalions) and dragged the slaughter out five days longer on an island only one-third the size of Guam.

The 77th InfDiv sent a number of reconnaissance patrols into southern Guam to verify there were no significant enemy forces in the area. MajGen Geiger wished to ensure the Corps rear area would be secure for the advance north. A stockpile of 13 days' supplies was built up to support the drive of two divisions north. The problems with difficult terrain were compounded by an extremely limited inland road and trail system on northern Guam, making forward movement, logistics, and evacuation extremely difficult. To this point IIIAC had lost 989 KIA, 302 MIA, and 4,836 WIA, with large numbers lost to exhaustion, illness, and non-combat injuries.

On 30 July MajGen Geiger ordered the 3rd MarDiv and 77th InfDiv to pursue the retreating Japanese on the morning of the 31st (W+10). The two divisions would swing north pivoting on Agaña with the 3rd on the left and the 77th on the right. The O-1 Line was the IIIAC's objective for 31 July, a line beginning at the east end of Agaña, running south to Famja Village, then to the Pago River and following it to the east coast. The attack was launched in the morning against little resistance. The 3rd Marines on the north flank advanced well beyond the O-1 Line securing the two main

After the flag raising at the Marine Barracks on 29 July, Marine leaders pose with one of the two bronze plaques recovered amid the wreckage, left to right: LtCol Alan Sharpley (Commander, 4th Marines; former Commander, 1st Raider Regiment), BrigGen Lemuel C. Shepard (Commanding General, 1st Prov MarBde), Col Merlin F. Schneider (Commander, 22nd Marines), and LtGen Holland M. Smith (Commanding General, Expeditionary Troops and FMF, Pacific). This plaque is today on display at the Marine Corps Historical Center, Washington, DC.

roads running north. 3/3 Marines faced no opposition in securing ruined Agaña, the island's capital. The 21st and 9th Marines halted at the O-1 Line for the night with the Division covering between two and five miles (3.2–8.1km). The dense nature of the vegetation and the light resistance saw the battalions bivouacking for the night in tight perimeters between a mile and 1 ½ miles (1.6–2.4km) apart. The 77th InfDiv's much wider swing east covered almost 10 miles (16.1km). The 307th Infantry was inland and the 305th advanced toward the east coast, reaching it at Pago Bay with virtually no resistance to secure its portion of the O-1 Line. On

Orote Peninsula's prize, the Japanese-built 4,500ft (1,372m) Orote Airfield. The light area above and to the left of the airstrip is the grounds of the Marine Barracks. To its immediate left, on lower ground alongside Apra Harbor, is Sumay, not apparent here. The first US aircraft landed on the field on 30 July.

Troops of 1/305 Infantry march inland to secure the Force Beachhead Line. This is typical terrain on southern Guam where the hill and ridge tops were covered with low scrub brush and grasses. The valleys and other low ground were usually choked with dense vegetation and trees.

the south side of the Pago River 2/307 discovered 2,000 Guamanians abandoned by the Japanese in a forced labor camp. 2/305 and the 77th Reconnaissance Troop screened the Division's exposed south flank and supply routes. The 1st Prov MarBde and the 306th Infantry secured the FBL and patrolled the island's southern portion.

The next day's advance continued to the O-2 Line running from the north end of Agaña Bay, just short of the Tiyan Airfield, then southeast to a point about a mile below Fadian Point on the east coast. Motorized patrols mounted on jeeps, halftracks, and tanks preceded the infantry during the advance on the few roads. The Japanese had emplaced hundreds of mines on roads and likely infantry routes, which slowed the advance more than actual enemy resistance. Some motorized patrols were forced to turn back because of the mines and aerial bombs rigged as mines. Off road movement was extremely difficult in most areas because of the density of the underbrush. The O-2 line was achieved by nightfall on 1 August (W+11), again with almost no opposition. In the center of 3rd MarDiv zone the 9th Marines were pinched out of the line and, for the first time since landing, the Division had a full regiment in reserve, although it was unlikely it would be needed as the Japanese were incapable of significant counterattacks by this time. The Marines secured Tiyan Airfield and the Army captured the Pago River bridge intact. Resupply was a major problem for the 77th; its supply dumps were 16 miles (27km) to the rear and there were no roads crossing the island west to east to serve as main supply routes. Engineers began bulldozing a road across the island, but it was feared that by the time it was completed it would no longer be needed as the advance would quickly outpace its construction. The speedy securing of the O-2 Line did provide a road from the rear, and although the delivery of supplies remained slow, work on the planned road was abandoned. The now congested Agaña–Pago Bay Road served both the 3rd and 77th Divisions and IIIAC Artillery. Although a two-lane, hard-surfaced route, it was overused, poorly maintained, and, with frequent rain, soon deteriorated

A 77th InfDiv rifleman clips M1 rifle rounds in a typical two-man foxhole on the Force Beachhead Line. It was often not possible to dig deeper holes because of the underlying layer of limestone.

A platoon of M4A2 tanks of the 3rd Tank Battalion rolls forward to support the 21st Marines in the center of the Northern Beachhead. Both the Marine and Army tank battalions and the two separate Marine tank companies on Guam used diesel-powered M4A2 Shermans.

badly. Engineers could not properly maintain the road and still allow the essential supply convoys through. The widely scattered units and dearth of roads and trails meant many units did not receive timely resupply of rations and water but, because of limited contact with the enemy, ammunition was not a problem.

The main Japanese line was eight miles (12.9km) north of the O-2 Line. Geiger desired to regain contact with the enemy as soon as possible to keep the pressure up and give him as little time as possible to prepare defenses. The advance was resumed on the morning of 2 August to the O-3 Line four miles to the north. This line stretched from the north end of Tumon Bay southeast across the island. The 307th Infantry encountered stiff resistance forward of the crossroads village of Barrigada and this would hold up the advance. Critical to the operation was the capture of the village's reservoir as water supply was becoming an acute problem. There were no streams on northern Guam and truck transport was mainly allocated to ammunition and rations, with little room for water and few water trailers. The 77th InfDiv sent out a light tank company in the morning before the general infantry advance began. The tanks passed through San Antonio advancing some 800yds (732m) before they made contact. They withdrew to report the enemy's location and then advanced on Barrigada where the column turned northwest toward Mt. Barrigada and Finegayan. They met resistance near the mountain and after destroying a small Japanese force returned to Barrigada. They then moved northeast until making contact 1,000yds (914m) beyond Barrigada. The tank patrol again withdrew and an approximate idea of the location of the Japanese lines was provided to the infantry. The infantry met strong resistance as they advanced into these areas. The 77th's advance halted for the day as enemy positions were reconnoitered further, but on the left the 3rd MarDiv made better progress pushing further ahead than the 77th. As a result, 2/21 Marines was attached to the 9th Marines to protect its exposed right flank. The advance continued the next day (W+13), but fighting was still heavy in the Barrigada area and confused all along the line as Japanese rearguards were

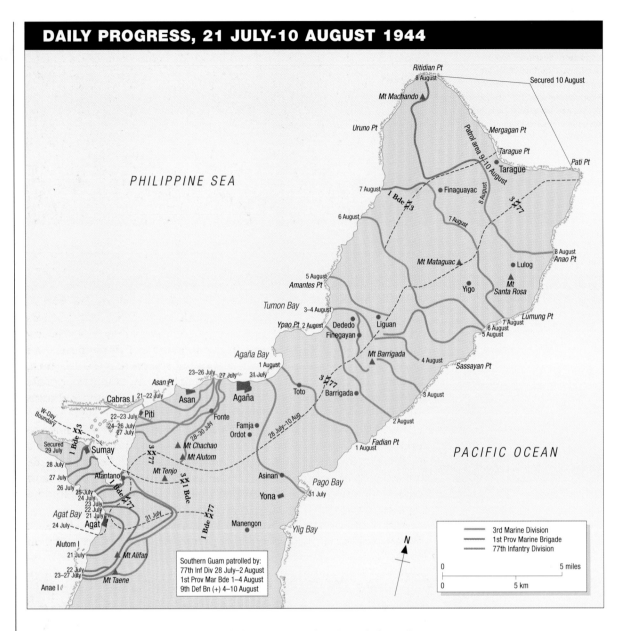

cleared out. The 3rd MarDiv achieved the O-3 Line, but it took from 3 to 5 August to clear Finegyan after a tough fight leaving over 700 Japanese dead. The right flank of the Marine line was still refused as the 307th faced increasing resistance between Barrigada Village and Mt. Barrigada. Yet further to the right the 305th pushed further north. Dense foliage, rough terrain, rain, sticky red mud, and water shortages hampered all units, but Mt. Barrigada was secured with little resistance, nevertheless. On 4 August the lead elements of four Marine Aircraft Group 21 fighting squadrons flew into refurbished Orote Airfield. They would take over day and night combat air patrols from the Navy. Navy aviation though would continue to provide close air support to the ground forces, a reversal of doctrinal roles between the two air services.

After the hard fights for Finegyan and Barrigada, the Japanese began falling back to the Mt. Santa Rosa stronghold. Geiger ordered a pursuit

3rd MarDiv troops seek what little cover is provided on the ridge tops overlooking the Northern Beaches. This was a common characteristic of Guam's hills and ridges, dense vegetation on the slopes, but near bare crests.

to commence immediately. Again, time was of the essence in order to keep up the pressure and allow the enemy less time to prepare additional defenses. The goal was to reach the O-4 Line just short of Mt. Mataguac and Yigo Village by 6 August (W+16). The 3rd MarDiv, with all three regiments once again in the line, pushed to within 1,000–1,500yds (914–1,372m) of the O-4 Line. Average company strength was so low that all units had to be placed in the line as the island's north end widened. The failure to retain a substantial reserve was, by this time, not an issue as the Japanese were incapable of mounting a credible counterattack. In the Army zone the 306th Infantry on the right was held up at Ipapao by diehard Japanese defenders, but the 305th on the right reached O-4. Japanese tanks still conducted small infantry-supported counterattacks in ones and twos and small pockets inflicted a small but steady dribble of casualties on American units. Because of wide unit frontages, dwindling strength, and the thick vegetation, units were seldom in contact with those on their flanks. Numerous Japanese were by-passed or slipped through the gaps.

As the Americans pushed north the island continued to widen and, with low unit strength and fewer troops needed to secure the south, on

3rd MarDiv troops moving north up the coast pass Japanese Type 95 (1935) 37mm gun-armed light tanks knocked out by Shermans. Of the 38 Japanese tanks on Guam, fewer than a third were 57mm gun-armed medium tanks.

the morning of the 7 August the 1st Prov MarBde was placed in the line to the left of the 3rd MarDiv. In anticipation, the Brigade had moved forward into assembly areas around Dededo by 6 August. All of IIIAC's under-strength regiments were lined up across the island left to right: 22nd, 4th, 3rd, 21st, 9th, 306th, 307th, and 305th. The end was finally in sight and the major push north would begin on 7 August (W+17).

Patrolling the South

With the FBL secure and the bulk of IIIAC forces pushing the tattered remnants of the enemy north, Geiger was still concerned that some enemy units may have withdrawn south and would pose a later threat to the rear area. The task of checking the south of the island initially fell to the 77th InfDiv. The island's south end consisted of jungle-covered hills and ridges plus two large inland swamps in the southeast. There were few roads and trails.

Between 28 July and 2 August the 77th Reconnaissance Troop sent seven five-man patrols, accompanied by Guamanian guides, to reconnoiter southern Guam. They found only a few scattered stragglers. Coupled with the fact that aerial reconnaissance revealed nothing, Geiger was assured no organized resistance remained in the south and he could send the 77th InfDiv north. The 1st Prov MarBde secured the FBL and took over responsibility for the south. From 1-4 August the Brigade sent out a number of long-range, platoon-size patrols, which found only empty defensive positions where II and III/10 IMR and III/38 Infantry had been located prior to the US landing. A 4th Marines patrol discovered a group of 2,000 Guamanians who were sent to the refugee camp established near Agat. Army Civil Affairs military government personnel were caring for the civilians providing food, shelter, and medical care.

The 2/305 Infantry digs in on Maanot Ridge just north of Mt. Alifan. The first Army unit to see combat on the island, it blocked Harmon Road leading to the Southern Beaches.

TOP, RIGHT **This Battery C, 7th 155mm Gun Battalion** crew cleans the bore of its 155mm M1A1 gun, a detail requiring all hands. This battery was initially attached to the 1st Prov MarBde during the landing. Note that board covers protect the hydraulic recoil cylinders. These were susceptible to shell fragments.

BELOW, RIGHT **1st Battalion, 19th Marines** engineers erected this cable tramway to evacuate wounded off Fonte Plateau. It was easier on the wounded than a jolting ride on hand-carried litters and much faster.

BOTTOM **An Army 105mm** battalion moves inland. Engineers built this road as a supply route beginning near Agat running northeast across the island to Yona, but it was only one-third completed before being abandoned. Existing roads further north were secured on which to move supplies, and the terrain proved too rugged to complete the road in time for it to be useful.

The 1st Marine War Dog Platoon was attached to the 1st Prov MarBde's 4th Marines; the 22nd Marines did not possess war dogs. The 2nd and 3rd Marine War Dog Platoons were attached to the 3rd MarDiv. War dogs, mostly Doberman Pinschers, served as scouts and messengers. Twenty-five died on Guam.

With the Brigade preparing to move north to complete the occupation of Guam, the 9th Defense Battalion was assigned responsibility for the south to include the defense of the FBL. With no air threat materializing and the 14th Defense Battalion securing Apra Harbor, the 9th reorganized as a rifle unit. For this mission the 9th headed a task force comprising 1/22 Marines and the Army's 7th AAA Battalion. The 9th conducted mounted and dismounted patrols in the south killing a number of stragglers and assisting Guamanians in hiding back to the refugee camp. Guamanians actively served as guides for the Army and Marines as well as providing a great deal of intelligence information. Throughout, despite the majority losing their homes and their livelihoods, the Guamanians remained resolute and loyal to America. Almost 1,000 are believed to have died during the fighting.

3rd MarDiv troops move up the coastal Agaña-Piti Road during the advance north. Marine troops can usually be differentiated from Army because the Marines wore camouflage helmet covers and the Army did not. This was not the case on Guam where few Marines used camouflage covers.

THE FINAL PUSH (W+17 TO W+20)

The Corps attack was launched at 07.00hrs on 7 August, with the Marines encountering light opposition and advancing as much as 5,000yds (4,572m) in some areas, 2,000 in others. Mt. Mataguac in the 9th Marines' sector proved to be lightly defended. However, it was not swept thoroughly and "bitter-enders" including LtGen Obata, remained on the hill. The majority of the Japanese resistance encountered took the form of scattered roadblocks; however, even at this late stage a few tanks were still encountered. The 77th InfDiv experienced resistance around Yigo Village in the morning, but this was quickly overcome. There was some confusion regarding the boundary between the 3rd and 77th Divisions. The Army was apparently unaware of corps orders shifting it to the west, despite the fact that it was clearly indicated in the corps operation order. However, the Army battalion advancing into the Marine zone was redirected before this caused a major problem. As aircraft, artillery (seven battalions), and naval gunfire blasted Mt. Santa Rosa, the Army regiments were in position to launch their attack on this last strongpoint at 12.00hrs. The advance was slow with numerous pockets of resistance encountered and the Division halted for the night short of the low hills in front of Mt. Santa Rosa. Counterattacks were expected during the night, but while some took place, they were small and ineffectual.

The 8 August attack was a continuation of the previous day's operation. The 1st Prov MarBde was responsible for the island's north end and east to Taraque Point. The Marines encountered such light resistance, with the jungle providing the most, that no effort was made to maintain contact between battalions. The end of the day found battalions widely separated and sitting astride the few roads and trails just short of the coast. Some patrols did penetrate to the sea, with a 22nd Marines patrol reaching

While Orote Airfield was placed in operation within days, Agana Field, built over the former Japanese Tiyan Airfield, required extensive reconstruction. It was two months before fighters of Marine Aircraft Group 21 could use the field.

TOP, LEFT **77th InfDiv troops march north during the pursuit of the battered Japanese. This was on central Guam's narrow isthmus. The density of the foliage increased as the troops advanced north.**

BOTTOM, LEFT **These unprotected 105mm M2A1 howitzers of the 3rd MarDiv attest to the fact that the Japanese had lost all their artillery during the retreat north and counterbattery fire was not a concern.**

BELOW **307th Infantry troops advance north toward Mt. Santa Rosa, the final Japanese stronghold. The tanks are M4A2 Shermans of the 706th Tank Battalion.**

Ritidian Point, Guam's extreme north end. The 3rd MarDiv in the center stopped $1^1/_2$ miles short of the coast, however, mainly because of the dense jungle. The 77th InfDiv concentrated on reducing Mt. Santa Rosa on the east coast. The 306th Infantry swung to the north of the hill to cut off escape into the dense jungles toward Piti Point. The 307th conducted an enveloping assault on the hill itself moving up its north and south flanks, while the 305th secured low hills on Santa Rosa's south side. Although it was feared that the remnants defending the area might number as many as 3,000 troops, few were found, most having already melted into the jungle. Santa Rosa was secured at 17.15hrs with only 500 Japanese dead found there. There was some confusion on 8 August over the use of roads and trails by the different units, but this was sorted out. With all the regiments in the line there were just not enough roads and trails for supply and evacuation vehicles.

The advance continued at 07.30hrs on 9 August. Five Japanese tanks and an infantry force had attacked before dawn causing 2/3 Marines to withdraw without casualties. By this time no one was willing to be the last to die on Guam. They reoccupied their positions at daylight and advanced on schedule. The 1st Prov MarBde consolidated its hold over the north end while the 3rd MarDiv advanced to within 1,500yds (1,372m) of the coast with the jungle again providing the stiffest resistance. Two Japanese light tanks were knocked out and seven medium tanks were found abandoned without fuel. The 77th InfDiv patrolled throughout its zone and found no organized opposition.

Patrolling was continued by all units on 10 August (W+20) with the same results – no organized resistance. At 11.31hrs MajGen Geiger declared Guam secure. The same day Admirals Nimitz (Pacific Fleet) and Spruance (Fifth Fleet) and Generals Smith (Expeditionary Troops) and Vandergrift (Commandant of the Marine Corps) arrived aboard the USS *Indianapolis* (CA-35).

Mopping-up continued and small groups of Japanese continued to harass the victors. Two Japanese officers, LtCol Takeda Hideyuki (Operations Officer, 29th Division) and Capt Sato (Commander, 24th Tank Company), attempted to organize resistance groups, but the demands of day-to-day survival, the search for food and water, lack of weapons, and constant American patrols left them hardly more effective than stragglers and other survivors. American patrols killed small numbers every day and others surrendered, but an estimated 7,500 Japanese were still at-large on the island when it was declared secure. The 3rd MarDiv and 77th InfDiv established a straggler line across the island from just above Tumon Bay to Fadian Point to prevent survivors from filtering south where they could harass the rear area and pillage food. The 77th organized three motorized reaction forces to deal with any enemy opposition south of the straggler line. On 10 August 1/306 attacked the final stronghold on Mt. Mataguac. It was overrun on the 11th and LtGen Obata is believed to have committed suicide that morning after sending a farewell message to Japan. Without doubt Japanese organized resistance had now ended.

Changes in command occurred rapidly once Guam was declared secure. LtGen Smith departed for Hawaii to assume his duties as Commanding General of the recently organized FMF, Pacific. MajGen Geiger and the IIIAC staff also departed on 12 August for Hawaii to prepare for the Peleliu operation leaving MajGen Turnage in temporary command

FEEDING THE "LONG TOMS" (pages 84–85)

III Amphibious Corps Artillery deployed a single 155mm gun battalion to Guam, the 7th. The 155mm M1A1 "Long Tom" gun (1) evolved from the French-designed G.P.F. M1917 and M1918M1 used in World War I. The M1A1 was standardized in June 1941. The M1A1 possessed a longer barrel, larger propellant chamber, and a modernized breech and firing mechanism. The M1 carriage (2) in particular was an improvement allowing high-speed towing and rapid emplacement and limbering. The Marines originally adopted the "Long Tom" in early 1943 to replace the 5in. Mk 15 Mod 0 and 155mm M1918M1 guns in the coast defense role. As the Japanese lost their ability to mount counterlandings and naval bombardment raids the 155mm soon came to be used for fire support on the frontline. With a range of 25,395yds (14.42 miles/23.22 km) it was ideal for counterbattery fire and long-range interdiction. Its crew of 15 could maintain a steady rate of fire of one round per minute; thus a four-gun battery could maintain a barrage with one round landing on the target every 15 seconds. For short durations a crew could pump out three rounds per minute. A three-battery battalion could deliver a barrage with rounds detonating almost continuously. The crew consisted of the section chief (sergeant) (3) wearing a Navy Mk 2 "talker" helmet plugged into the battery fire control telephone net over which he received the fire mission, gunner (corporal) (4), assistant gunner (corporal) (5), ammunition corporal, three ammunition handlers (6), eight cannoneers, and two truck drivers (the entire crew is not visible in this scene). The prime mover was a 2½-ton 6x6 short wheelbase cargo truck to which the gun's trails were attached to an M2 two-wheel heavy limber (7). Ammunition included the M101 high explosive (8) and M104 white phosphorus smoke (9) weighing 94.70lbs and 98.18lbs, respectively. A 30.74lb charge (10) propelled the high explosive projectile, which, depending on the angle of impact, had a 30 x 50yd (27 x 46m) bursting area, fragments reached as far as 360yds (329m). Both point detonating and mechanical time fuses were used, the latter enabling airburst shells to be fired that were devastating to troops in the open or in open-topped trenches. The 155mm gun battalions were formed in the spring of 1944 by detaching the two-battery 155mm seacoast artillery group from defense battalions, which were converted to AA battalions. While intended mainly for fire support, the new gun battalions still retained the coast defense mission. The M112B1 armor-piercing round was available for anti-ship use. This round could penetrate 5.8–6.8ins. (14.7–17cms) of armor at 500yds (457m) and several feet of reinforced concrete, allowing it to be used in the direct-fire role against fortifications. (Howard Gerrard)

A typical Marine patrol base near Ritidian Point. Such bases supported the mopping-up of the island's north. Security was not an issue as the surviving Japanese were leading a hunted existence.

of the assault troops. All units on Guam were turned over to VAC on 13 August when MajGen Harry Schmidt and his staff arrived. Island Com-mand, Guam under MajGen Larsen, had taken command of Orote Peninsula and Cabras Island on 2 August to begin base development, namely the airfield and seaport. It assumed formal command of Guam on 15 August. Island Command grew rapidly as it took over all logistics, construction, and civil affairs tasks in stages. It included the 5th Naval Construction Brigade with the 27–29th Seabee Regiments with 12 Seabee, four Army, and one Marine engineer battalions plus "Lion 6", a Navy advance base force responsible for building and operating Naval Operating Base, Guam. Island Command was also responsible for the care of 21,000 Guamanian civilians and built replacement housing for 15,000. Both the 3rd and 77th Divisions maintained an infantry regiment and an artillery battalion in the north to deal with diehards. Up to 80 Japanese were killed each day during the first two weeks after Guam was declared secure. The nightmare would continue for the Japanese for some time to come. The 3rd MarDiv took over sole responsibility for island defense under Island Command on 22 August. The 1st Prov MarBde departed for Guadalcanal on 31 August, where it would be expanded into the 6th MarDiv to fight on Okinawa. The 3rd MarDiv remained on the island to train for Iwo Jima, as did the 77th for Leyte and later Okinawa.

---

9 Four and a half companies of IJN rifle troops and laborers, with one company detailed to Mt. Mataguac.

AFTERMATH

In August 1944, Guam was the second most costly Marine Corps operation of the war to date, with Saipan (11,727 casualties) first; and Guadalcanal third (4,420 casualties). The Corps' losses in the forthcoming Peleliu operation would be only marginally less than on Guam. Iwo Jima and Okinawa would far exceed these operations. Total casualties on Guam by service were 6,734 Marines, 843 soldiers, and 245 sailors. Not included in the US casualty table are 18 Marines and four soldiers listed as MIA. Most Marine battalions lost over 300 killed each, some almost 500. The regiments suffering the highest casualties were the 21st (1,390), 22nd (1,147), and 3rd (1,075) Marines. The 9th Marines and 4th Marines lost 963 and 912, respectively. The Army regiments had comparatively light casualties (305th – 345, 306th – 130, 307th – 237). Besides the dead and wounded, large numbers of men were lost to combat and heat exhaustion, dengue fever, and dysentery, the latter two afflicting most of the troops on the island. Some of these were returned to duty as were some wounded. No replacements were received during the battle other than the 1st Prov MarBde's inadequate 394-man replacement company.

An inordinate number of accidental bombing and misdirected artillery incidents caused numerous friendly casualties. Some considered close air support to be less than adequate. Among the reasons for this and the friendly bombing and artillery casualties were the inaccurate maps with insufficient terrain detail and constant air-to-ground communications difficulties experienced by the joint assault signal units whose responsibility it was to request, control, and direct air, artillery, and naval fire support.

Table: US Casualties

Unit	KIA	DOW	WIA	Total
STLF/IIIAC Troops	63	14	204	281
IIIAC Artillery	5	5	57	67
3d MarDiv (+)	738	255	3,244	4,237
1st Prov MarBde	368	96	1,600	2,064
Navy medical in Marine units	43	3	180	227
77th InfDiv (+)	177	–[10]	662	839
Island Command, Guam	10	3	48	61
Navy shore elements	3	0	15	18
Total	*1,407*	*376*	*6,010*	*7,794*

Japanese casualties can only be estimated. With approximately 18,700 IJA and IJN troops on Guam, when the island was declared secure the body count amounted to some 10,971 dead. Many more were buried in pillboxes, bunkers, and caves. For each American killed in action 11 Japanese died. US forces claim to have knocked out 59 Japanese tanks,

[10] Included in the KIA figure.

but there were only 38 on the island; obviously more than one unit claimed killing the same tank.

The hunt for Japanese stragglers was relentless and without mercy. On no other island were there so many unorganized stragglers. One group of 35 men under Capt Sato surrendered on 11 June 1945, almost 10 months after the battle. By the end of August 1945 18,337 Japanese dead had been counted, 1,250 prisoners captured, and approximately 500 Japanese civilians interned. A POW camp was established at Sumay. These figures amount to more than the numbers of Japanese present on the island, especially when considering that hundreds or even thousands more were buried in fortifications and not counted. The body count was probably inflated. On 4 September 1945 LtCol Takeda surrendered with 68 men. A few individuals capitulated in 1960, with one last soul, Corporal Yokoi Shoichi of the 38th Infantry, finally surrendering in January 1973. This is near miraculous as the US units staging on the island conducted extensive combat-training patrols. The Marine Corps-advised Guam Combat Patrol and Guam Police hunted Japanese diehards for years simply for "sport."

Most existing Apra Harbor port facilities had been destroyed and the towns of Agaña, Sumay, and Piti leveled. Piers were built on Cabras Island and the harbor bottom dredged. Guam was struck by a typhoon in October and much of the new port construction was destroyed, but soon rebuilt. The breakwater was extended to more completely protect the harbor. Naval Operating Base, Guam became a major cargo port, repair facility, and submarine base. An extensive island-wide permanent road construction project was also undertaken. Among the extensive island-wide road projects was a 12-mile long (19km) packed coral road connecting Agaña and Sumay; the first four-lane highway in the Pacific. Numerous supply depots, hospitals, and troop camps were built. Guam became a major staging base for the planned invasion of Japan.

The airfield on Orote Peninsula was designated Navy Airfield, Orote. North and Northwest Airfields, each with two B-29 bomber runways, were built near Ritidian and Pati Points and were operational in February and

June 1945, respectively. It was from North Field that the first B-29 raid on Japan was launched from the Marianas on 24 February 1945. Agana Field was built over the Japanese Tiyan Airfield and used by transports with a second runway later added. Harmon Field, initially named Depot Field, was built to the north of Agaña on the site of the cleared Japanese Dededo Airstrip. XXI Bomber Command was headquartered there from December and then the Twentieth Air Force from July 1945, where it remained until May 1949. Agana Field was then turned over to the Navy and redesignated Naval Air Station, Agana.

ORDERS OF BATTLE

DECEMBER 1941

Naval Forces, Guam

Governor, Guam, and Commandant, Naval Station, Guam	Capt George J. McMillin (USN)
Aide for Civil Affairs to Governor, Guam and XO, Naval Station, Guam	Cdr Donald T. Giles (USN)
CO, Navy Yard, Piti, Guam	LtCdr O.W. Gains (USN)
CO, Marine Barracks, Sumay, Guam	LtCol William K. McNulty (USMC)
XO, Marine Barracks, Sumay, Guam	Maj Donald Spicer (USMC)
Guam Insular Patrol	1stLt Charles S. Todd (USMC)
USS *Penguin* (AM-33)	Lt J.W. Haviland, III (USN)
USS *Robert L. Barnes* (AG-27)	Lt J.R. Nestor (USN)
Navy Hospital, Agaña, Guam	Capt W.T. Lineberry (USN)

Japanese Forces

South Seas Detachment	MajGen Horii	
HQ, 55th Infantry Group		109
144th Infantry Regiment	Col Kusonose	2,925
I Battalion, 55th Mountain Artillery Regiment		773
3rd Company, 55th Cavalry Regiment (+ AT gun platoon)		96
1st Company, 55th Engineer Regiment		269
Other Attachments		734
Company, 47th Field AA Gun Battalion		
Detachment, Medical Unit, 55th Division		
Detachment, 1st Field Hospital, 55th Division		
Detachment, Water Supply Unit, 55th Division		
5th Company (+), Maizuri 2nd SNLF	Cdr Hayashi	370

JULY–AUGUST 1944

Southern Attack Force (TF 53)	Rear Adm Richard R. Conolly[11]
Northern Attack Group (TG 53.1)	
Northern Transport Group (TG 53.3)	Capt Pat Buchanan
Minesweeping and Hydrographic Group (TG 53.9)	LtCdr G.M. Estep
Tractor Group 3 (TG 53.16)	Capt G.B. Carter
Southern Attack Group (TG 53.2)	Rear Adm L.F. Reifsnider
Southern Transport Group (TG 53.3)	Capt J.B. McGoven
Tractor Group 3 (TG 53.17)	Cdr E.A. McFall
Minesweeping and Hydrographic Group (TG 53.6)	Cdr R.R. Sampson
Corps Reserve Group	Capt H.B. Knowles
Carrier Support Group (TG 53.7)	Rear Adm V.H. Ragsdale

III Amphibious Corps (Southern Troops and Landing Force – TG 56.2)
Force Troops
    IIIAC Service Group [shore party and services]
    IIIAC HQ&S Battalion (-)
    IIIAC Signal Battalion (-)
    4th Marine Ammunition Company
IIIAC Artillery
    1st (-) and 2nd 155mm Howitzer Battalions
    7th 155mm Gun Battalion
IIIAC Rear Echelon
    1st Base Headquarters Battalion
    1st Separate Engineer Battalion
    1st MP Company
    3rd Joint Assault Signal Company
    5th Field Depot (-)
1st Prov Base HQ, Island Command, Guam
    HQ&S Battalion, 1st Prov Base HQ

3rd MarDiv (Reinforced)
3rd Combat Team [Beaches "Red 1" and "Red 2"]
    3rd Marines (Reinforced)
    25th NC Battalion (-)
    Company C, 1st Battalion [engineer], 19th Marines
    Company F, 2nd Battalion [pioneer], 19th Marines
    Company C, 3rd Medical Battalion
    Company C, 3rd MT Battalion
    Company C, 3rd Tank Battalion [M4A2]
    Battery I [40mm], Light Antiaircraft Group, 14th Defense Battalion

---

11 Commander both Southern Attack Force and Northern Attack Group.

9th Combat Team [Beach "Green"]
  9th Marines (Reinforced) [1/9 Division Reserve]
    1st Battalion [engineer] (-), 19th Marines
    3rd Tank Battalion (-) [M4A2]
    Company D, 2nd Battalion [pioneer], 19th Marines
    Company G (+ detachment, HQ Company), 25th NC Battalion
    Company A, 3rd MT Battalion
    Company A, 3rd Medical Battalion
    3rd Reconnaissance Company (-)
21st Combat Team [Beach "Blue"]
  21st Marines (Reinforced)
    2nd Battalion [pioneer] (-), 19th Marines
    Company B, 1st Battalion [engineer], 19th Marines
    Company H (+ detachment, HQ Company), 25th NC Battalion
    Company B, 3rd Medical Battalion
    Company B, 3rd MT Battalion
12th Marines [artillery] (Reinforced)
  14th Defense Battalion (-)
Reserve Group
  HQ Battalion (-), 3rd MarDiv
  Company B (-), 3rd Tank Battalion [M4A2]
Engineer Group [shore party]
  19th Marines [engineer] (-)
  2nd Separate Engineer Battalion
  25th NC Battalion
  Company B, 2nd Special NC Battalion
Service Group
  3rd Medical Battalion (-)
  3rd Service Battalion (-)
  Detachment, Service Group, 5th Field Depot
  2nd Marine Ammunition Company (-)
Attachments
  1st Armored Amphibian Tractor Battalion (-) [57 x LVT(A)1]
  3rd Amphibian Tractor Battalion (+) [193 x LVT(2)/(4)]
    Company A, 10th Amphibian Tractor Battalion [LVT(2)]
  IIIAC MT Battalion (-) [60 x DUKW]

1st Prov MarBde
HQ Company, 1st Prov MarBde
MP Company, 1st Prov MarBde
Signal Company, 1st Prov MarBde (-)
1st Prov Replacement Company
4th Combat Team [Beaches "White 1" and "White 2"]
  4th Marines (Reinforced)
  Engineer Company, 4th Marines
  Medical Company, 4th Marines
  MT Company, 4th Marines
  Pioneer Company, 4th Marines
22nd Combat Team [Beaches "Yellow 1" and "Yellow 2"]
  22nd Marines (Reinforced)
  Engineer Company, 22nd Marines
  Medical Company, 22nd Marines
  MT Company, 22nd Marines
  Pioneer Company, 22nd Marines
  Tank Company, 22nd Marines [M4A2]
305th Regimental Combat Team (USA) [Brigade Reserve]
  305th Infantry Regiment (Reinforced)
  242nd Engineer Combat Battalion [shore party]
  Company A, 302nd Engineer Combat Battalion
  Company C (-), 706th Tank Battalion [M4A2]
Artillery Group, 1st Prov MarBde
  HQ Detachment, Artillery Group, 1st Prov MarBde
  Pack Howitzer Battalion, 4th Marines
  Pack Howitzer Battalion, 22nd Marines
  305th Field Artillery Battalion (105mm Howitzer) (USA)
  Battery C, 1st 155mm Howitzer Battalion
Amphibian Tractor Group
  4th Amphibian Tractor Battalion (+) [178 x LVT(2)/(4)]
    Companies A and B, 1st Armored Amphibian Tractor Battalion [26 x LVT(A)1]
    Company A, 11th Amphibian Tractor Battalion [LVT(2)]
    Company C (Amphibian Truck), IIIAC MT Battalion [40 x DUKW]
Antiaircraft Group
  9th Defense Battalion (- Seacoast Artillery Group)
  Battery A, 7th AA Automatic Weapons Battalion [40mm/.50-cal.] (USA)
IIIAC Medical Battalion (Reinforced)

77th Infantry Division (Reinforced) (- 305th RCT to 1st Prov MarBde)
Divisional Troops
HQ, 77th Infantry Division
Special Troops
  HQ Company, 77th Infantry Division
  77th Cavalry Reconnaissance Troop
  77th Signal Company (- detachments)
  77th Quartermaster Company
  777th Ordnance Light Maintenance Company (-)

HQ and HQ Battery, 77th Infantry Division Artillery (-)
  306th Field Artillery Battalion (155mm Howitzer)
  306th Regimental Combat Team
  306th Infantry Regiment (Reinforced)
  304th Field Artillery Battalion (105mm Howitzer)
  132nd Engineer Combat Battalion [shore party]
  Company B, 302nd Engineer Combat Battalion
  Company B, 706th Tank Battalion [M4A2]
  Company B, 302nd Medical Battalion
  Battery B, 7th Antiaircraft Automatic Weapons Battalion
307th Regimental Combat Team
  307th Infantry Regiment (Reinforced)
  902nd Field Artillery Battalion (105mm Howitzer)
  233rd Engineer Combat Battalion [shore party]
  Company C, 302nd Engineer Combat Battalion
  Company A, 706th Tank Battalion [M4A2]
  Company B, 302nd Medical Battalion
  Battery C, 7th Antiaircraft Automatic Weapons Battalion
Attachments
  7th Antiaircraft Automatic Weapons Battalion (-) [40mm/.50-cal.]
  302nd Engineer Combat Battalion (-)
  302nd Medical Battalion (-)
  36th Medical Field Hospital (-)
  95th Medical Portable Surgical Hospital
  Company A (-), 88th Chemical Battalion (Motorized) [4.2-in. mortar]
  292nd Joint Assault Signal Company (-)
  404th Ordnance Medium Maintenance Company

Japanese Forces, Guam

29th Division (-)[1] (Southern Marianas Army Group)

29th Division HQ	220
18th Infantry Regiment (- I Battalion)[2]	1,300
38th Infantry Regiment	2,894
29th Division Intendance Unit	133
29th Division Signal Unit	186
29th Division Ordnance Unit	45
29th Transport Unit	94
24th Tank Company	117
265th Independent Transport Company	180
Element, HQ, 13th Division[3]	200

1. 50th Infantry Regiment on Tinian.
2. I Battalion on Saipan. Strength further reduced by submarine losses.
3. Advance detachment probably absorbed into other headquarters.

48th Independent Mixed Brigade (-)

48th IMB HQ	149
319th Independent Infantry Battalion	368
320th Independent Infantry Battalion	486
321st Independent Infantry Battalion	488
322nd Independent Infantry Battalion	500
48th IMB Artillery Unit	368
48th IMB Engineer Company	186
48th IMB Signal Company	109
48th IMB Medical Company	164
2nd Company, 9th Tank Regiment	122

10th Independent Mixed Regiment (-)*

10th Independent Mixed Regiment (-)*	1,912
10th IMR HQ	
II Battalion	
III Battalion	
10th IMR Artillery Unit (-)*	
10th IMR Engineer Company (-)*	
10th IMR Signal Company	
1st Company, 9th Tank Regiment	122

* I Battalion, an artillery company, and an engineer platoon on Rota.

52nd Field Antiaircraft Battalion (- 1st and 3rd Co)	250
Antiaircraft Unit, 18th Infantry	
45th Independent Antiaircraft Company	
2nd Company, 7th Independent Engineer Regt	225
2nd Company, 16th Shipping Engineer Regt	200

IJN Forces, Guam

54th Guard Force	2,300
21 coast defense gun companies	
60th Antiaircraft Defense Unit	259
217th Construction Battalion	900
218th Construction Battalion	900
Land Reclamation Unit (civilian laborers)	300
Guam Branch, Southeast Area Air Depot	100
263rd Air Group (*Hyo* Unit)	800
521st Air Group (*Otori* Unit)	400
755th Air Group (*Genzan* Unit)	700

Harmon Field was built on the site of the incomplete Japanese Dededo airstrip north of Agaña. XXI Bomber Command was headquartered there from December and **Twentieth Air Force from July 1945. Each of the five US airfields built on Guam was massive compared to the three crude airstrips built by the Japanese.**

THE BATTLEFIELD TODAY

Guam remained an important naval base after the war. One post-war role was the trials of 44 Japanese war criminals. Permanent facilities construction and improvements continued through the post-war years. On 30 May 1946, the US Naval Government was re-established. Headquarters for US Naval Forces, Marianas, sat atop Nimitz Hill on the west side of Agaña and was the administrative center for the US Commonwealth of the Northern Marianas and the US Trust Territories of the Pacific Islands. US Army, Mariana and Bonin Islands, was also headquartered on Guam. Camp Witek, now closed, was established at Talofofo to house Marine units until 1949. Naval Operating Base, Guam, was redesignated Naval Base, Guam, in 1952, then Naval Station, Guam, in 1956, becoming a ballistic missile submarine homeport. Naval Air Station, Guam, remained operational, the old Orote Airfield, which is now only used for Marine helicopter operations. Naval Supply Depot, Guam, is located around Apra Harbor. From 1965 to 1972, B-52 bombers flew missions to Vietnam from Andersen Air Force Base, renamed from North Field in 1947. Northwest Field is now know as Andersen Northwest and serves as an auxiliary airfield designated Naval Facility, Guam. Guam housed over 100,000 Vietnamese refugees in 1975 and 6,600 Kurdish refugees from Iraq in 1996. In 1995 Naval Air Station, Agana, was closed and became the Antonio B. Won Pat International Airport.

Naval administration ceased in September 1949 and Guam was transferred to the Department of the Interior, with a local governor elected at that time. Guamanians were granted American citizenship in August 1950 and it became the Territory of Guam *(Teritorion Guam)*. The island is an organized, unincorporated territory of the United States with its own local government. It is under the jurisdiction of the Office of Insular Affairs, Department of the Interior. In 1962 Guam's ports were opened to foreign visitors. Today the capital of Agaña is officially called Hagatña, but the old name remains in wide use.

Tourism is a major industry on Guam and it provides a complete support infrastructure including the full range of hotels, restaurants, car rental, tour and recreational services. The majority of the visitors are from Japan, South Korea, United States, and Taiwan. The second largest industry is the government, to include employment by the Navy.

The War in the Pacific Historical Park (http://www.arizonamemorial.org/warinpacific.html) is operated by the US National Park Service and encompasses six sites: 1: Asan Beach with gun casements, caves and pillboxes, plus 445 water acres of reefs and relics. There is a memorial to the units participating in the landing overlooking the Asan Beaches. 2: Around Asan Village are caves, pillboxes, entrenchments, and a 75mm mountain gun. 3: Piti Navy Yard area has three Japanese coastal defense guns. 4: Mounts Chacho and Tenjo have a pre-World War II US gun emplacement and offer hiking with beautiful views. 5: Mt. Alifan has caves and tunnels; bomb and shell craters are along the winding hiking trails. 6: The Agat area provides underwater relics and unspoiled reefs. There are over 1,000 acres of submerged relics and sunken ships accessible to scuba divers and snorkelers. The German cruiser SMS *Cormoran* was scuttled in Agat Harbor in 1917 when America entered World War I. The troop transport *Tokai Maru* and freighter *Kitsugawa Maru* also lay on the harbor's bottom. The Marianas Military Museum is located on the Naval Station and is open to the public. A Marine Corps war dog cemetery for the 25 dogs killed on Guam is located on Orote Point. The South Pacific Memorial Park is located at Mt. Mataguac in the north. Its 50ft (15m) granite monument and museum commemorate the Japanese troops lost in the Marianas. "Tweed's Cave" can be found on the northwest coast where George Tweed hid out for over two years. Numerous Japanese guns and deteriorating fortifications can be found scattered all over the island. Additionally, there are scores of historical sites representing the Spanish colonial and ancient Chamorro periods.

BIBLIOGRAPHY

Arthur, 1stLt Robert A. and Cohlmia, 1stLt Kenneth. *The Third Marine Division.* Washington, DC: Infantry Journal Press, Inc., 1948. (Battery Press reprint available)

Cass, 1stLt Bevan G. *History of the Sixth Marine Division.* Washington, DC: Infantry Journal Press, Inc., 1948. (covers 1st Prov MarBde) (Battery Press reprint available)

Crowl, Philip A. *United States Army in World War II: Campaign in the Marianas.* Washington: US Government Printing Office, 1960.

Fuller, Richard. *Shokan – Hirohito's Samurai: Leaders of the Japanese Armed Forces 1926–1945.* London: Arms and Armour Press, 1992.

Gailey, Harry. *The Liberation of Guam: 21 July–10 August 1944.* Novato, CA: Presidio Press, 1997.

Lodge, Maj O.R. *The Recapture of Guam.* Washington: HQ Marine Corps, 1954. (Battery Press reprint available)

Morison, Samuel E. *History of US Navy Operations in World War II: New Guinea and the Marianas, March 1944–August 1944, Vol. VIII.* Boston: Little, Brown and Company, 1958.

Myers, Max (editor). *Ours to Hold High: The History of the 77th Infantry Division in World War II.* Washington: Infantry Journal Press, 1947.

O'Brien, Cyril J. *Liberation: Marines in the Recapture of Guam.* Washington Navy Yard: History and Museums Division, Marine Corps Historical Center, 1994.

Rottman, Gordon L. *US Marine Corps Order of Battle: Ground and Air Units in the Pacific War, 1939-1945.* Westport, CT: Greenwood Publishing, 2002.

———— *World War II Pacific Island Guide: A Geo-Military Study.* Westport, CT: Greenwood Publishing, 2002.

Sankei Shimbun Fuji. *The Last Japanese Soldier: Corporal Yokoi's 28 Incredible Years in the Guam Jungle.* London: Tom Stacey Ltd., 1972.

Shaw, Henry I. Jr. Nalty, Bernard C. and Turnbladh, Edwin T. *History of US Marine Corps Operations in World War II: Central Pacific Drive, Vol. III.* Washington: US Government Printing Office, 1966.

Stanton, Shelby L. *Order of Battle, U.S. Army, World War II.* Novoto, CA: Presidio Press, 1984.

Tweed, George R. as told to Clake, Blake and Givens, D. Turner. *Robinson Crusoe, USN: The Adventures of George Tweed, RM1, USN on Japanese-held Guam.* New York: McGraw-Hill, 1945. (Book on which the 1962 motion picture *No Man is an Island* was based. Reprint available from Guam: The Pacific Research Institute, 1995.)

War Department. *Guam: Operations of the 77th Division, 21 July–10 August 1944.* Washington, DC: War Department, 1946.

INDEX

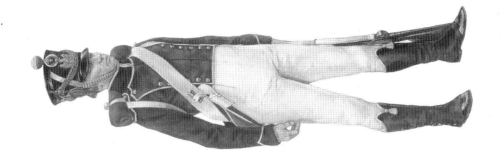 

FIND OUT MORE ABOUT OSPREY

❏ Please send me the latest listing of Osprey's publications

❏ I would like to subscribe to Osprey's e-mail newsletter

Title / rank

Name

Address

City / county

Postcode / zip   state / country

e-mail

CAM

I am interested in:

❏ Ancient world
❏ Medieval world
❏ 16th century
❏ 17th century
❏ 18th century
❏ Napoleonic
❏ 19th century

❏ American Civil War
❏ World War 1
❏ World War 2
❏ Modern warfare
❏ Military aviation
❏ Naval warfare

Please send to:

USA & Canada:
Osprey Direct USA, c/o MBI Publishing, P.O. Box 1, 729 Prospect Avenue, Osceola, WI 54020

UK, Europe and rest of world:
Osprey Direct UK, P.O. Box 140, Wellingborough, Northants, NN8 2FA, United Kingdom

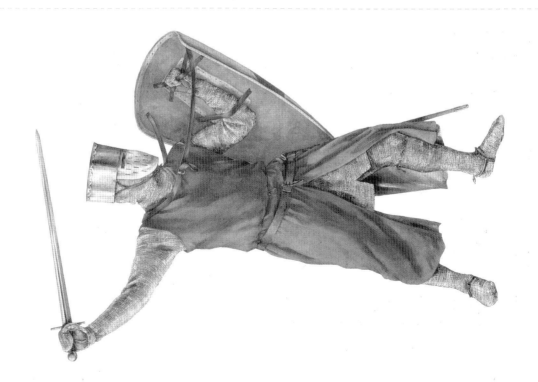

OSPREY
PUBLISHING

www.ospreypublishing.com

call our telephone hotline
for a free information pack

USA & Canada: 1-800-826-6600
UK, Europe and rest of world call:
+44 (0) 1933 443 863

Young Guardsman
Figure taken from *Warrior 22:*
Imperial Guardsman 1799–1815
Published by Osprey
Illustrated by Richard Hook

Knight, c.1190
Figure taken from *Warrior 1: Norman Knight 950 – 1204 AD*
Published by Osprey
Illustrated by Christa Hook

POSTCARD